WATERLOO
YOU NEVER KNEW

JOANNA RICKERT-HALL

WATERLOO
YOU NEVER KNEW

Life on the Margins

DUNDURN
PRESS

Editor: Dominic Farrell | Designer: Laura Boyle
Cover image: Geoffrey Hayes, *Waterloo County: An Illustrated History, 1997*

Library and Archives Canada Cataloguing in Publication

Title: Waterloo you never knew : life on the margins / Joanna Rickert-Hall.
Names: Rickert-Hall, Joanna, 1955- author.
Description: Includes bibliographical references and index.
Identifiers: Canadiana (print) 20190090367 | Canadiana (ebook) 20190090375 | ISBN 9781459742901 (softcover) | ISBN 9781459742918 (PDF) | ISBN 9781459742925 (EPUB)
Subjects: LCSH: Waterloo (Ont.) | LCSH: Waterloo (Ont.)—Social life and customs. | LCSH: Waterloo (Ont.)—History. | LCSH: Waterloo (Ont.)—Social conditions.
Classification: LCC FC3099.W39 R53 2019 | DDC 971.3/45—dc23

Canada Council for the Arts | Conseil des arts du Canada
Canada
ONTARIO ARTS COUNCIL
CONSEIL DES ARTS DE L'ONTARIO
an Ontario government agency
un organisme du gouvernement de l'Ontario

We acknowledge the support of the Canada Council for the Arts and the Ontario Arts Council for our publishing program. We also acknowledge the financial support of the Government of Ontario, through the Ontario Book Publishing Tax Credit and the Ontario Media Development Corporation, and the Government of Canada.

Printed and bound in Canada.

Dundurn Press
Toronto, Ontario, Canada
dundurn.com, @dundurnpress

For my mother, Phyllis, whose love of history inspired my own, and for Anne Marie, a Waterloo County gal who loved a good story

CONTENTS

FOREWORD

LIVES LIVED ON THE EDGES of settlement, where definitions can blur even as fresh insight increases understanding, gave compelling shape to the Waterloo County that is Joanna Rickert-Hall's storied land. In this book she deftly pulls her readers into a marginal zone. Once there, where energy and imagination jostle, she shapes a vibrant portrait of "ordinary people who lived in extraordinary circumstances."

In her carefully crafted account, across two hundred years, the contours of analysis are fresh and the lives depicted strongly rooted in the county's past. Guiding us through boundary territory, the author introduces a range of individuals described as transient, such as the poor or criminals, in contrast to lives marked by conventions at the centre of settlement. In the course of her investigation, she finds dynamic patterns that have influenced the region across time and, through her focus on margins, she notices new energies.

Waterloo has a richly configured history with layers of interpretation on library shelves that have enticed generations to explore its pathways. Rickert-Hall builds on this scholarship and pushes further to reveal unfamiliar figures and facets of local history. Her perspectives, both as scholar and teacher, have given her a vibrant sense of the structure of the region. So comfortable is she in the archives that her work easily pulls us into Waterloo's past, often along unmarked trails. So too her years as an historic site interpreter, uncovering the past to visitors of all ages, has honed her storytelling skills. Sensitive to what visitors want to know and what they need to know, she occupies her terrain with a cache of artifacts and storied lives at hand.

Further sustaining Rickert-Hall's passion for the culture of Waterloo County is her background in anthropology, cultural planning, museum studies, and heritage concerns. From these several disciplines, she brings to her rendering of Waterloo's past a profound understanding of the character of the place as it has been forged over time. If you have seen Joanna's welcoming smile when she is in period costume, you will sense the adventures that await you on these pages. Her lively and wonderfully detailed account offers an analysis of the pressures of time and change that have moved across the surfaces of Waterloo — the city, the township, the county, and the region.

Stephanie Kirkwood Walker
February 2019

PREFACE

YOU MIGHT SAY THE DEAD TALK TO ME. Every story in this book tells the tale of someone who has died. To me, their presence lingers, begging to be heard. Through these accounts, whether previously told or not, their stories have been left behind in death records, newspaper articles, and diaries. These beckon to me. To hear them, one must be willing to listen. And, one must be willing to dig into strange places.

These stories need telling, and I admit that I feel compelled to tell them. These are not my stories or my personal journey, but I feel that someone must share them. So, I am beginning the process that those more worthy may take up the torch and go where I cannot. These stories have often been obscured or forgotten because of their marginality. *Marginality*, in this book, is the term used to describe the condition of the people who live apart from the mainstream, by choice or by design. Some may have lived their lives on the margins of society because they were unable to gain access to the important things in life, but others chose an existence that defied social conventions, doing so for personal reasons or for profit.

Waterloo County House of Industry and Refuge. This black-and-white sketch of the house was published in the *Canada Illustrated News*, March 23, 1872. The House had opened in 1869.

This book introduces stories of ordinary people who lived in extraordinary circumstances — touched by disease, poverty, crime, and, arguably, even the supernatural. These are stories many communities own but may not share (at least publicly) — scandals, murder, passion, and greed. No one story sums up the total of a community's identity, but collectively they speak to the complex tableaux of layered existence within any (and, arguably all) communities. Our history is your history.

Some of those mentioned in this book lived their lives in infamy, while others only found that at the ends of their lives. Many possessed multiple social identities, moving between the varied strata of social status and privilege. Consider, if you will, the politician whose fascination with séances was so strong that it affected not only his personal life but also his professional one. Great pains were taken to conceal his activities from the general public in order to protect his reputation and his ability to perform his job.

There is also the once-esteemed doctor who fell from grace by robbing the dead in their final repose. These were men of high social status, seemingly respectable, yet their secret actions and interests forced them to hide parts of themselves from society.

Others, many of whom were far less fortunate, nonetheless left their own marks on the history of this community. There is the story of the ex-slave who lived a long but otherwise unremarkable life in obscure poverty. In the end, disabled and elderly, he died a pauper's death in the Waterloo County House of Industry and Refuge. That would have normally been the end of his story — but he was rescued from obscurity after his death, when local residents who respected him greatly published his obituary (not once but twice), poignantly recognizing him as someone "nearly every citizen" knew. There is another story that highlights the apparent contradiction between traditional Mennonite spiritual beliefs and the practice of occult healing. And so it goes. These stories, however fraught with emotion, outrage, or scandal, need to be told and need to be remembered. It is through their telling that we meet the people who were most affected by the arbiters of policy and law-making (either by breaking the law or by being contained by it). An encounter with the mundane and ordinary lives of the past enables us to hold up a mirror and see ourselves.

A note about "life on the margins," marginalism, and marginalization: it is prudent to remember that the language we use does matter. A margin is defined as a boundary that demarcates one thing from another. In discussions of social status, those described as "marginal" are thought to live, act, behave, or believe in things other than those considered to be the norm for the society. The marginal whose stories are told in this book lived lives — by choice or because of social prejudice — outside the social mores commonly accepted at the time (some of these have sociocultural parallels and conventions that are still in effect today).

The types of margins that we create illuminate how we perceive what we see, and what we (think) we know or "understand." To truly understand a society, whether one existing today or one existing in the past, it is necessary to examine the nature of the margins created — what is (or was) considered "beyond the pale."

Stigma is attached to those deemed "different," to those whom society has marginalized, and judgment of them precludes worthiness, as in the case of ideas surrounding "able-isms"(what people can or cannot do) and poverty — the deserving poor (worthy of "help") and the undeserving poor (those deemed not worthy). Those deemed unworthy are most often the social pariahs, the outcasts whose stories are subsumed within a large narrative, in which their identities and the rationale for their actions are rendered invisible, having only symbolic value within the bigger social picture. It is curious, though, that at the same time such people are deprived of their individuality — they are lumped into a marginalized group — they often lose the right to privacy, too. In order for such marginalization to occur, some aspect of a person's identity must be thrown into the spotlight. In effect, they become commodified products or "public property," worthy of scorn, moral scrutiny, or criticism (perceived as not capable or willing to care for themselves). They are sometimes pejoratively categorized as the "burdens of society." The perpetuation of socioeconomic and political biases that are directed toward the most vulnerable among us is often the toxic result of "othering" (looking at others as "them," not me or us, and thinking of them as if "they" are inferior). Able-ism, age-ism, racism, and even "religious-ism:" most of these categorizations are contextual and based on circumstantial identifiers like status, race, colour, or creed. Food for thought.

The stories in this book, while filled with curious and entertaining characters, also provide an impetus for the reconsideration of social labelling as a useful tool, particularly when we encounter the real people behind their real "histories." As you'll discover in this book, people can move within social categories, either "up" or "down" — sometimes at will and sometimes forced by decisions and circumstances beyond their control. The way such movements are viewed is made clear in the language used to describe them: falling from grace, getting back upon one's feet, rising above one's station, putting one's life back together, falling in with the wrong crowd, facing the court of public opinion, etc. In the process of discovering historical "facts," we, too, must consider the language (and the assumptions behind the language) that we use when we analyze and process them. How well we do that will depend upon the philosophical lenses we choose to use.

Waterloo You Never Knew: Life on the Margins considers the bigger questions: where do we see ourselves in these stories, and in what ways do we in modern times understand those who did (and did not) fit the "norm" historically. And, are we really that different from those in the past?

This book offers an accessible opportunity for us to examine disparate life histories that could, in many ways, be those of any community: the forgotten, the poignant, the funny, and the downright strange. We also get the chance to see behind the curtain of polished conventionality, cleaned up for public consumption. One may call it the "real deal" — warts and all. *Our* history is *your* history.

The book is divided into five sections (with an Epilogue providing contextual synthesis and conclusion). Part One, "Life on the Margins," considers the history of Waterloo County, focusing on the occupation, governance, and development of the land prior to the arrival of the Pennsylvania German Mennonites. (The use of the term *Pennsylvania Dutch* in relation to the German-speaking settlers who came to Waterloo County from the United States, although common in everyday speech, is incorrect. They were not "Dutch"; rather, they were German-speaking. It is believed that the name is really a corruption of the word "Deutsch," the German word for themselves. Throughout this book I use the term "Pennsylvania German" to describe them.)

Chapter 1 introduces the backstory of land development in and around Waterloo County following the Revolutionary War. The area was once a vast, old-growth forest, occupied and relatively unchanged for centuries by the Indigenous Peoples who lived here. During the war, a controversial colonial settlement strategy forged between Joseph Brant and the British Crown changed everything.

Chapter 2 presents the accounts of strangers and transients, and the sociopolitical effects of "othering" within a rural Ontario context that was isolated by both geography and the perceived lack of potential economic opportunities. In 1834 the Galt cholera epidemic wiped out a large portion of the region's pioneer families. This tragic event left an indelible mark on the young community, affecting the ability of the survivors to provide for themselves or their families. Widowed fathers often married widowed mothers of deceased family members and friends (or vice versa). Others took in orphaned children and adopted them. The surviving community had to pick up the pieces.

As the social landscape evolved, we see in Chapter 3 the arrival of the area's first black ex-slaves, whose stories define the very meaning of marginal existence. Here we explore the significant contributions they made during their tenure in the area — the first barber in Berlin (today, Kitchener) was also a Queen's University law graduate and a man with a love of Shakespeare, who ran for public office. From nothing, the black community in Waterloo County built churches and schools to educate their children in the hope of a better life in a new land. The questions remain: how were they treated and what eventually happened to them?

Part Two, "Containment," examines the various institutions built throughout the nineteenth century to "contain" or restrict the freedom of those who were considered to be disposable, unruly, or, in some cases, public property. Chapter 4 examines the dichotomy between the desire to care for the vulnerable and marginalized and the persisting attitude toward who is considered worthy (or not) to receive such assistance. In many cases, then and now, those who need the support are not those who benefit from it. The criteria used to decide who fit into these categories were broadly defined and subjective. By the nineteenth century, attitudes toward the indigent (the homeless), the mentally ill, and orphaned children were becoming more sympathetic, yet prejudices still lingered. For example, those down on their luck were divided into the "deserving poor" and the "undeserving poor." Those deemed "undeserving" were left in desperation to fend for themselves, and so faced the uncertainties of life on the streets or, in the worst-case scenarios, some form of incarceration. Even those poor who did receive some assistance faced miserable and uncertain lives.

The Waterloo County Gaol (1852–1978) was the holding tank for many in transition — whether or not they had actually committed crimes in the conventional sense. In Chapter 5 we see that justice was not always equally dispensed, particularly in the case of those convicted of addictions (alcoholism was a rampant social concern, especially among the mentally ill, the indigent, and the poor), of "promiscuity," and of known violent crimes. Consider the story of the father who approached the local authorities to incarcerate his sixteen-year-old daughter who refused to marry — on the grounds that he was worried that, if she did not marry, she would fall into a life of ill repute. This story reveals, in stark detail, the contrast between the prevailing attitudes toward "unruly" (read, "promiscuous") women and those toward men. It must be noted that the ultimate punishment, execution, was given only to men. Three hangings took place at the Gaol, and all were of males who had been convicted of murder.

Chapter 6 considers the ways in which Waterloo County responded to the increasing demand for the care and confinement of those who could not otherwise care for themselves. The Waterloo County House of Industry and Refuge operated from 1869 to 1950, providing institutionalized housing and medical care to the most vulnerable and marginalized residents of the area. Known as "inmates," the residents of the House of Industry and Refuge were comprised of the area's most disadvantaged men, women, and children. Their ages ranged from newborn to debilitated (and often senile) seniors. Separated by sex and age within the walls of the poorhouse,[1] some had family members who could not (or didn't want to) provide care for them in life. More poignant still are the stories of what happened to those who went unclaimed, by family or friends, after death. Chapter 7 presents the stories of those most vulnerable of all — orphaned or abandoned children.

Part Three, "Dodgy Dealings and Risky Business," takes a turn away from institutional care and containment and looks at life from the criminal's point of view. Here, the perpetrators are not from disadvantaged or vulnerable backgrounds. Instead, it may be argued that by occupying conventional social positions their privilege allowed them the opportunity to opt for a marginal existence by choice (and certainly for profit). Chapter 8 examines the notorious side-life of at least one local bootlegging business during Prohibition. Reputedly, at least one Mennonite courier was employed to keep quiet and haul goods to secret locations outside of Waterloo where they would be picked up and shipped Stateside.[2] Are these myths or reality?

Ask Allan Buehler, whose diary account describes the shady business dealings that took place after hours at a local garage where few questions were asked.

In Chapter 9, the story of a good doctor gone bad details the rise and fall of Dr. Frederick Christ, a once-respected physician in 1850s Waterloo County. His lucrative foray into the messy business of bodysnatching for profit might have remained secret had it not been for the mysterious smells that emanated from his residence. What finally brought him to justice? His shameless and drunken bragging in a local tavern. After a stint in the Waterloo County Gaol in 1859, the doctor returned to his practice, seemingly none the worse for wear — except for the suspicion that he may have poisoned both of his wives and caused one of them to die by suicide. This chapter truly reveals facts that are stranger than fiction.

Part Four, "In the Devil's Snare," enters the realm of the supernatural and examines beliefs and practices in Waterloo County during the nineteenth and early twentieth centuries. Chapter 10 introduces the topic of a curious folk-medicine tradition known as "charming" that was once condoned and practised among Pennsylvania German settlers who brought it with them when they relocated to Waterloo County. This practice borrows from a number of sources, relying heavily on ancient Judeo-Christian occult magic texts and Biblical teachings. It also drew on knowledge of plants and their uses. Those who practised this form of "medicine" were not conventionally trained physicians; rather, they were widely recognized as people who possessed a "God-given" gift that enabled them to heal the sick in ways that were sometimes perceived as witchcraft. Christian Eby, for example, was a controversial Mennonite charmer whose reputation and practice during the latter nineteenth century and early twentieth exceeded geographic boundaries well beyond Waterloo County. To date, the practice of charming has been widely studied in Europe and the United States, but little has been written about its presence in Canada, particularly among the Pennsylvania German diaspora who settled in Waterloo County.

Chapter 11 provides a unique look into the spirit world of psychic mediums and those who engaged their services. Although some psychics have certainly been debunked as fraudulent hucksters, others have provided great comfort to their clients by offering them something otherwise unattainable: the possibility of contacting their beloved dead. High-profile clients like Prime Minister William Lyon Mackenzie King and artist Homer Watson were fervent believers and frequent clients of mediums. The prolific Maines-Pincock family of mediums, who taped and photographed their séances, claimed they had proof of spectral activity. Over the years of their practice, they captured and compiled hundreds of eerie photographs that show dazzling sprays of light, called ectoplasm, surrounding their clients in session. Finally, we examine the curious case of nurse-turned-psychic Vera McNichol, whose particular skills (helping clients to find lost people and things) were not only popular with police services but had international ramifications. Incidentally, McNichol was named by Ottawa as "Canada's Only Official Clairvoyant." Although she lived in neighbouring Perth County, she grew up in Kitchener and many of her clients were from the greater Waterloo area.

In Part Five, "History as Storytelling," the stories presented are reviewed. The reader is asked to consider the notion of choices: the choices we make and the choices that are sometimes made for us. This book provides numerous examples of people who lived on the margins of social convention, whether by choice or by design. Many of the lives presented, particularly those of people from economically, physically, and mentally marginalized populations, have been glossed over or even obscured in mainstream histories. But it must be remembered that what has been obscured or hidden is nevertheless important in the historic record of a community and its social boundaries. Each soul contributes a thread to the tapestry of a community's identity. Some of these threads are shiny, expensive, and glossy; others are faded and almost invisible — yet, they are there, awaiting discovery.

Welcome to *Waterloo You Never Knew: Life on the Margins.*

PART ONE

Life on the Margins: Cultivating Community

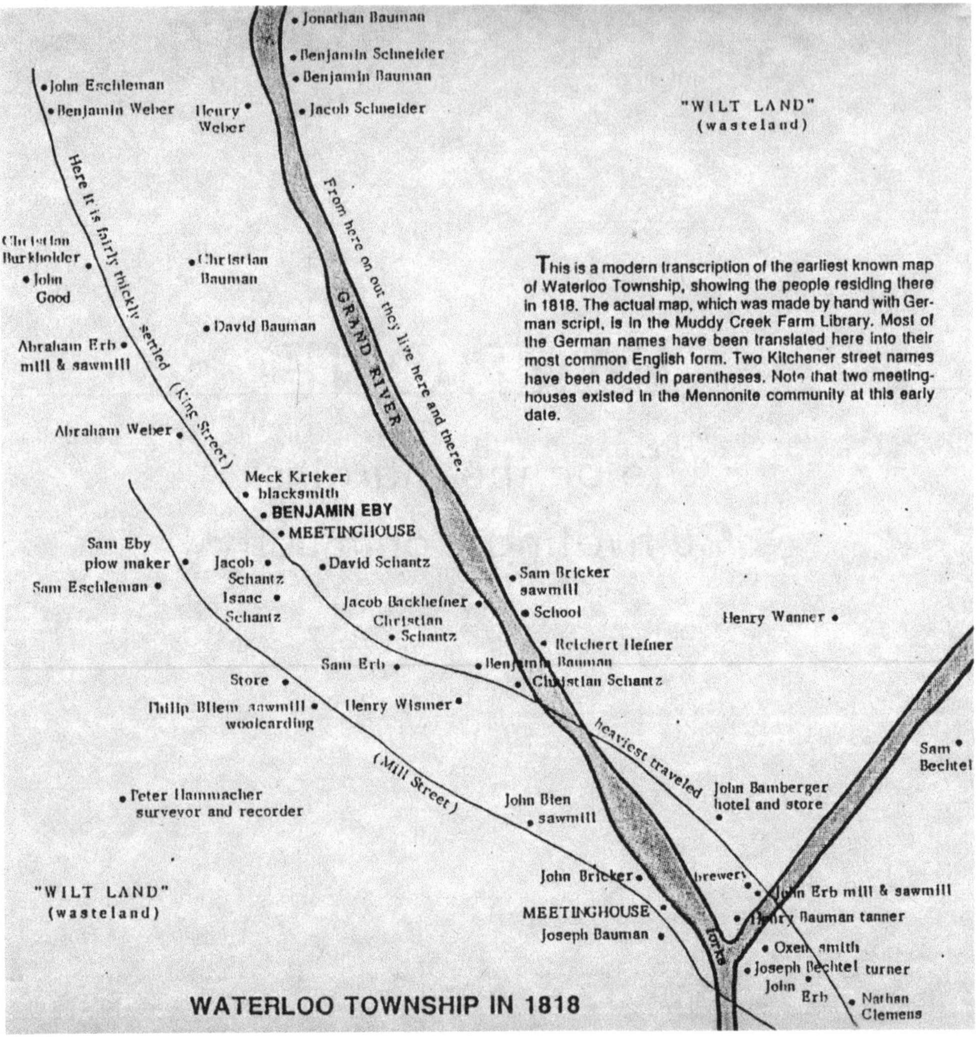

This is a modern transcription of the earliest known map of Waterloo Township, showing the people residing there in 1818. The actual map, which was made by hand with German script, is in the Muddy Creek Farm Library. Most of the German names have been translated here into their most common English form. Two Kitchener street names have been added in parentheses. Note that two meetinghouses existed in the Mennonite community at this early date.

WATERLOO TOWNSHIP IN 1818

1

WATERLOO COUNTY IN HISTORICAL CONTEXT

Those in power write the history, while those who suffer write the songs.

— Frank Harte

A SEARCH FOR LAND

As the numbers of European settlers and their U.S.-based descendants increased in Lower Canada (modern-day Ontario) during the eighteenth century, the Indigenous Peoples of the province found themselves competing for natural resources and land in what had once been their traditional hunting and seasonal settlement territories. To control and potentially mitigate conflict with the colonists, King George III issued the *Royal Proclamation of 1763*. In its simplest sense, the Proclamation was designed to effectively define the Crown's jurisdictional boundaries and accordingly reinforce its governance of its conquered land. This was not intended to permanently settle the issue, and yet the act stirred controversy — many of the settlers balked at the idea of sharing land with the Indigenous Peoples of the region. They were worried that they were now at risk of losing the land that had been granted to them by the Crown, because of the newly established territorial boundaries.[3]

Even modern historians disagree as to whether this legislation was detrimental or beneficial to later Indigenous land claims, suggesting that the British Crown was making a show of assuaging Indigenous concerns over the perceived encroachment of white settlers while at the same time increasing their own political control over the territory. This arguably lessened the Indigenous claims for land ownership in favour of the white settlers.[4, 5] Other historians believe that this Proclamation effectively recognized Indigenous Peoples' rights to claim the land that they occupied in a way that previous legislation had not considered, irrespective of the land claims of the white settlers.[6] The truth is that the boundary claims were anything but permanent. This lack of a solid resolution was ignored for the time being, however, since, within a few years, the British Crown had other concerns as it prepared for war with its American colonies. It now turned to the Indigenous Peoples for help.

JOSEPH BRANT AND THE LAND FOR THE SIX NATIONS RESERVE (1743–1807)

Joseph Brant, an influential Mohawk military leader, was not a full-blood Mohawk; however, he enjoyed life as a man who benefited from and existed between two worlds — both Indigenous and white — on reserve land. Many today recognize Brant's iconic Indigenous significance, both positive and negative, to the Six Nations Confederacy[7] — regardless of his ancestry or interethnic political associations.

He travelled to London, England, in 1775 to solicit support for his people in view of the pending war between the American States and the British Crown.[8] Although not a hereditary chief, Brant, as a result of his military office, had the prestige and status to be a powerful advocate for his people. In his role as military leader and translator, Brant seized upon an unprecedented opportunity that would have far-reaching historical effects. The deal Brant struck specified that if the Iroquois (also known as the

Haudenosaunee and the Six Nations Confederacy) fought in support of the British, the Crown would confer a land grant to them in Canada (or, as it was known then, the territory of British North America).[9] By 1783 Brant had selected the Grand River valley as the place where he and his people would like to settle. On October 25, 1784 (and at the direction of the Crown), Sir Frederick Haldimand issued the *Haldimand Proclamation*, effectively granting ownership to the Six Nations Confederacy, in deference to their military support for the British interests in the Revolutionary War, the land running six miles (ten kilometres) on either side of the Grand River valley along its length.[10] It should be noted, however, that Brant was not above reproach for his territorial gains from the Crown. In fact, he encouraged Loyalist friends of his from Butler's Reserve (with whom he had fought in the Revolutionary War) to settle with their families on the same reserve land, offering some of them larger land claims than those afforded to some other Six Nations settlers.[11] In 1798 Brant built himself a large two-storey home in the growing nearby settlement that took his name — Brantford. For the purposes of the later histories contained within this book, we are most concerned with Blocks 1, 2, and 3 of this tract.[12] That there were (and still are) ongoing disputes and misunderstandings concerning the divergent interests over this tract of land is a story well-documented and seeking resolution.

Suffice it to say, by the end of the eighteenth century, a growing group of Pennsylvania German farmers were looking for cheap land and Chief Joseph Brant believed he had the right to sell some of the land his people had acquired from the British Crown — 94,012 acres[13] and in May 1796, first evidence of this transaction between Brant, Philip Steadman Jr., Richard Beasley, and William Wallace (the attorney for Joseph Brant) was registered for the sale of Blocks 1, 2, and 3, accordingly.

The land that became Waterloo County was, for the most part, a heavily forested and lush region made up of old-growth trees and fertile soil. Indigenous people had selectively cleared some areas in the region, leaving pockets of open grassy areas where they established seasonal subsistence gardens and village settlements, and engaged in successful hunting and fishing. The Mississauga[14] had also established strategic pathways that enabled them to move from one camp to another — many of which eventually were co-opted to become some of the area's oldest roads. Mill Street in Kitchener, which ran beside what became known as Schneider Creek, is one such former trail.

PENNSYLVANIA COMES TO WATERLOO

Most of the early white settlers to this area were, as previously stated, Mennonite farmers — the descendants of Anabaptists who had settled in the Pennsylvania area nearly a century before. Having already established successful farming communities in Pennsylvania, the Pennsylvania Germans found that land had become increasingly scarce and more expensive as the eighteenth century progressed. By 1784 some of the frugal Mennonites who searched for cheaper land to purchase began to emigrate to the Canadian side of the Niagara Region, settling in Lincoln County, Ontario (in and around Vineland). What they found was lush land with fertile soil, and in time the community they built flourished and became known colloquially as "the Twenty," as it was established along the nearby Twenty Mile Creek, so-named because of the location of its mouth, which is twenty miles west of the Niagara River.

Word of their success spread to their friends and neighbours back home in Pennsylvania. Some of these countrymen had also heard of fertile land that was for sale north of the Twenty, and in 1799, accompanied by a native guide and surveyor, Jacob Bechtel and a group from Bucks County, Pennsylvania, arrived in Waterloo County to scout out the area to survey its settlement potential. They were quickly followed by Joseph Schörg (Sherk) and Samuel D. Betzner, who are often credited with being the first two settlers to the area.[15] Thus, in 1800 the influx of Pennsylvania German immigrants to Waterloo County began.

The journey they faced was long, slow, and arduous. Their passage through the Allegheny Mountains was difficult, and the group's heavily laden Conestoga wagons often got stuck and needed to be unpacked, pulled along, and then repacked. As they crossed by barge at Black Rock (modern-day Buffalo) over the Niagara River, they suffered many unforeseen hardships.[16] Along the way, the settlers battled thick mud (so deep that even dogs were lost in it); nearly impassable, bug-infested swamps; and forests that were filled with wild animals. At night, they slept in the woods in tents they had brought with them. Beyond Dundas, Ontario (the last outpost for supplies that they passed on their journey northward), there were no real roads. In fact, John Steckle points out that one "whole party spent about two weeks in making a corduroy road" through the dreaded Beverly Swamp just so they could get through it. Many of the settlers walked beside their wagons, roads or no, carrying tired children. The expedition took anywhere from four to seven weeks.

Once they arrived, the settlers' survival depended upon their ability to erect shelter and provide food for the upcoming winter months — there would have been no real crops to harvest in their first year. But most of all, their survival depended upon their faith in God and, of course, on each other.[17] It was said that in the first year following settlement, there was little food to spare and that even the peelings of potatoes were saved for planting the following spring. The potential for disaster was great, as were the real dangers of starvation and death.

Many of the Mennonite settlers kept journals and detailed their positive interactions with their Indigenous neighbours, who often could be found sleeping by the fire when the settlers awoke in the morning. Following a shared communal breakfast, they would exchange trade goods (Mennonite wives were known for their fresh baked bread, which was gladly offered in exchange for haunches of venison). Pioneers like Joseph Schneider's daughter Louisa fondly remembered the warm friendships that developed between them. As an old woman, Louisa mentioned that it had once been the custom of their Indigenous friends to bring gifts of handmade baskets to their home on New Year's Day when she was a young girl. These friendships may very well have ensured the settlers' ability to survive (and thrive) in their new homes.

Although such accounts are unarguably useful when trying to discover the truth about the past, it is important to read historical overviews with caution, as some of these writings record only the successes. "Pioneer life was crude and brutish for most people. For every founding family that prospered, there were at least ten times as many who failed," says historian Elizabeth Bloomfield. She tells us that we know less about the unfortunates and failures because they dropped out of township society and the local written record,

Christian Schneider homestead (built 1807) c. 1900.

moving back home or on to other settlement frontiers. Everyday tragedies like farming accidents, childbirth-related deaths, and disease claimed the lives of many family members and made more difficult an already tenuous existence. For those who stayed and those who managed to survive the odds of dying, diversifying their survival strategies became necessary coping mechanisms and perhaps the key to their success. In addition to their extended community of friends and family or *Freundschaft*, the Mennonites had a strong faith in God. They practised frugality and self-reliance, and, perhaps most importantly, they had an entrepreneurial spirit.

Many of the early settlers developed a secondary source of income that supplemented the money they received for the food they grew on their farms. For example, Mennonite pioneer Joseph Schneider[18] erected a sawmill in 1816, while others planted large orchards and set up cider mills in their emergent villages. W.V. Uttley, in his 1937 account *The History of Kitchener*, points out that the production and sale of alcohol was also a viable commodity for some, adding that Schneider's distant relation, "Indian Sam" Eby,[19] was a distiller of whisky.

It is no surprise that mills of one form or another were among the first types of commercial structures in the area, which was known for its good (and plentiful) watercourses. In the early days, these were the key source of power for mills. For farmers, the mills were also their early social centres. As Frank Epp notes, "As the farmers cleared the land they became lumbermen and established sawmills. As agriculture expanded and barley was introduced, breweries were added to the grist mills; both flour and alcoholic beverages were considered essential to the social economy of the day." Elizabeth Bloomfield observes, "a trip to the mill [often took] two or three days and [finding it] comfortable a farmer could meet other farmers] so that it became a social centre, and a business mart as well. They warmed their victuals and made coffee at the fireplace and slept on the floor or on the bags of bran."

Abraham Erb was one of these early Mennonite millers. He invested heavily in the area and became a successful entrepreneur. He has been credited as being the founding father of the Village of Waterloo. When he came to Canada from Pennsylvania in 1806, he owned approximately four thousand acres of land, which encompassed much of what was to become the City of Waterloo today. Following his brother John's[20] example in Preston, Abraham established a sawmill and grist mill on Beaver Creek, a western tributary of the Grand River (where present-day Waterloo Park is located). Erb continued to contribute to his growing community in a variety of ways — he donated land for its first schoolhouse and served as Waterloo Township's tax collector from 1822 until sometime before his death in 1830.

In time, each community within Waterloo County developed under the collective efforts of its respective constituency. Some of these settlements disappeared, as others merged into larger villages and towns. Some are still recognizable today, while others exist only as signs along the highway — a vague memory of a settlement that once was. What is certain, however, is that each contributed to the history of this region in its own way — perhaps not in the form of individuals' life histories, but more as the collective struggles that each faced in the quest for viability and longevity. As the region grew and prospered over time, so too did the problem of containing those who didn't quite "fit."

2

TRANSIENT ENTERTAINMENTS: A MENAGERIE (AND CHOLERA) COME TO TOWN

> Community, in its most general sense, means all the people who live in a place or settlement and who are usually linked by their everyday business contacts and needs for shared services.
>
> — Elizabeth Bloomfield, "Building Community on the Frontier: The Mennonite Contribution to Shaping the Waterloo Settlement to 1861"

BY THE SPRINGTIME OF 1834, things were looking up for the little village of Galt, Ontario. After many years of struggling to build a viable economy and attract new settlers to their community, the inhabitants were finally enjoying the rewards of their collective labour. It hadn't been an easy ride, but their perseverance had certainly paid off.

By 1821 the first tavern had appeared, offering simple accommodation for travellers passing through the area. In time, this was followed by connections to other larger communities — roads east to Guelph, south to Dundas (itself a trade nexus for the burgeoning pioneer agricultural market

Artist's rendition of the village of Galt in the early 1800s.

economy), and beyond, the roads to Hamilton and Niagara. The road north connected first with Preston, then Berlin, and, a bit farther away, Waterloo. The construction of these roads enabled travel to and from the area with greater ease. Galt was no longer an island, bounded by rivers and various watercourses. It was now connected with the outside world.

With backing from John Galt, the construction of businesses and homes flourished and these structures were soon complemented by the area's first churches — First Presbyterian Church in 1831 and St. Andrew's in 1833. Schools were another matter. Nearby Blair had founded the area's first school in 1802 (the Rittenhouse School), but Galt needed one of its own. As James Young describes it in *Reminiscences of the Early History of Galt*, the village's "first school, not erected until 1832, was a rough-cast "diminutive log building, situated where the Merchant's Bank now is" located at "the head of Main Street." By 1834 the population of Galt had reached upwards of two hundred souls.

Rural pastimes were few and far between in the early days. Following busy work days, events such as church picnics, occasional musical concerts, and imaginative games offered abidingly welcome entertainments for the common folk entrenched in their daily routines. So, it's little wonder that when the news of an impending visit from a travelling menagerie (often incorrectly reported as a "circus")[21] first hit Galt in the spring of 1834, locals could hardly believe their good fortune. Excited by the then unparalleled revenue and tourism opportunities, many locals welcomed the chance to host the exotic exhibition, scheduled for July 28, 1834.

What they didn't know was that death was heading straight for them. Within less than ten days after the performance, about one fifth of the greater community's population would be dead.

I have always considered it odd that written accounts of the 1834 Galt cholera epidemic paid particular attention to the arrival date of the "Showmen with a Menagerie" that preceded the outbreak. It seemed a bit sensationalistic to me to preface the narrative with this particular detail, even if it were technically true. Was the mention of the arrival of the travelling menagerie and its troupe an attempt to offload the blame for the disease onto the community's transient "outsiders"? Was it a way to avoid implicating the good citizens of Galt in what eventually happened (i.e., the actions and lack of action that increased the disease's ability to take hold of the unsuspecting attendees to the show)? It's hard to say.

So, what did happen?

Upon the arrival of the travelling menagerie in town, it was discovered that one of the showmen was displaying symptoms of cholera. Immediately, concerned citizens made their case to the magistrate, Absalom Shade, to shut the show down. Shade considered the pros and cons of letting the show go on, keeping in mind the financial benefits the show might bring to the community. Acting as the host of an exotic (and relatively high-profile) exhibition like this was an opportunity too tempting to pass up. Surely the citizens were overreacting? It couldn't be as bad as they were reporting, could it?

In the end, Shade decided that, since there was no proof that the performer actually had cholera, and since the benefits from hosting the event would be great, the show should be allowed to go on. So, a window of opportunity to shut down the show (and banish its ill showman) was lost. Had the show been cancelled, it's possible that the severity of the impact on Galt would have been lessened.

Before delving further into what happened and why, it's necessary to step back and look at both the disease and the nature of travelling menageries.

Cholera is an acute disease that is caused by a particular strand of bacterium known as *Vibrio cholerae*. Symptoms include bloody diarrhea. Typically, this depletes the body of massive amounts of bodily fluids within hours of contact, which usually causes the death of the victim shortly thereafter. The course of the disease is swift and deadly — cholera symptoms can present themselves in as little as two hours after exposure.

The bacteria flourish in warm water and humid conditions, and they are most often transmitted through ingestion of contaminated food and water. In an era where people did not wash their hands and had little to no knowledge of how to handle food safely, it is no surprise that the disease spread easily. Although cholera epidemics have resulted in the death of massive numbers of people, the disease is, in fact, preventable and also curable. Fluid replacement (clean water and electrolyte salts) are crucial when treating those infected and suffering in the active phase of the disease, yet a common treatment in the nineteenth century involved the withholding of water.

A one-time summer event of such excitement that it attracted large crowds and travellers from a fair distance would undoubtedly be the perfect venue for a disaster. To sensationalize the story, make that spectacular summer arrival an exotic exhibition of "Showmen with a Menagerie." Exotic, indeed.

Cholera, itself, is of ancient origin. Mention of it can be found in texts from fifth century BCE India. The Greek physician Hippocrates, writing in the fourth century BCE, described cholera-like illnesses that were affecting patients, with devastating results. In 1543 Gaspar Correa, a Portuguese historian, spoke of a disease that was moving through the Ganges delta, where it was rumoured that its victims developed life-threatening symptoms within only eight hours and succumbed a few hours later. In the early part of the nineteenth century, cholera was on the move. The disease vector was believed to be contaminated rice — a ubiquitous food staple. The outbreak travelled along trade routes that had already been established by seasoned European traders. By 1820 the disease had arrived in Thailand. As it continued to migrate, more than a hundred thousand succumbed on the island of Java alone. From there it moved to China, then westward from Asia into Europe. It is believed that the particularly harsh winter of 1823–24 helped to kill off the bacteria, but by 1830 it appeared, yet again, in Moscow. Spreading throughout Europe, *Asiatic cholera*, as it was then known, reached London in the spring of 1832.

Needless to say, rampant fear of the invisible assailant caused the general public great fear. Paranoia and distrust of those in authority — particularly the medical profession — was widespread. With no cure in sight, nor understanding of how the disease was spread, panic was a constant among the general public. Massive numbers of deaths meant massive numbers of burials and authorities were hard-pressed to keep up with their duty to the swiftly dispose of the victims, who were often buried together in mass graves for expediency's sake. Cholera pits, like the mass graves of medieval plague victims, were often unmarked. Sadly, even though victims' personal effects were fumigated and infected bodies regularly burned, gravediggers sometimes became infected themselves, from having come in contact. As a result, they, in turn, helped to spread the disease.

By 1832 cholera crossed the Atlantic Ocean, by way of various ships carrying feverish new immigrants (like the Irish ship *Carrick* that arrived in Montreal in June 1832). Three days after its arrival in port, the first cholera victim was reported. By the end of June, more than a thousand deaths were attributed to the disease in Quebec. In Montreal, lack of sewers and appropriate garbage disposal resulted in the contamination of city's water supply. In a very short time, the disease was out of control and deaths multiplied. Doctors did their best but were generally ill-prepared, overwhelmed, and ill-informed. There appeared to be no cure. It didn't help that the folk belief at the time attributed the disease's transmission to bad smells and bad air — also known as *miasma.* By the end of 1832, over nine thousand deaths in Lower Canada were associated with cholera. A short time later, the disease arrived in Upper Canada and, eventually, Galt.

Since ancient times, exotic animals have been kept captive by the rich and powerful as status symbols. Often they were given as gifts by foreign dignitaries to ruling monarchs. William the Conqueror kept a small menagerie of animals at his Woodstock residence, and sometime around 1100 his son Henry I enlarged the collection. By the twelfth century, King John founded the most prominent collection of captive animals at the Tower of London, and that became known as the Royal Menagerie (or Tower Menagerie), where over sixty different exotic species of animals were housed. The collection initially contained lions and bears, but over the years (and centuries) leopards, tigers, elephants, various monkeys, and hyenas were added. During the reign of Elizabeth I, the collection was opened to the general public and a small admission fee was charged. The English aristocracy were not the only ones to collect captive animals, however. Louis XV of France had a vast menagerie at Versailles, as did other European nobles in Italy, Spain, and Norway, to name a few. By 1831 32 the Tower Menagerie animals were transferred to the London Zoo, which, in its infancy at that time, was the first scientific zoo of its kind in the world. The zoo was opened to the public in 1847.

Commercial travelling exhibitions of captive animals in England appeared early in the eighteenth century and were accompanied by showmen who acted both as scouts for potential new shows and as trainers and handlers for the animals. Needless to say, housing and feeding the animals was an enormous task. They were also a highly expensive investment, so it was incumbent upon the showmen to book as many exhibitions of the animals as they could. Travelling menageries did not emerge until late in the eighteenth century in North America. It was not until 1796 that the first elephant came to the United States; it was followed by two tiger cubs in 1806 and a lion in Boston (1807). These menageries, known as "Museums of Living Animals," staged performances designed to satisfy more than mere curiosity. They were both entertaining and educational.

* * *

In the Upper Canada of the early nineteenth century, travelling menageries were not unknown, but the vast majority of these featured exhibitions of more abundant (and more cheaply obtained) species, such as bears, deer, and mountain lions that had been captured by hunters and farmers. These were most often shown outside of rural taverns and inns. In Berlin, Friedrich Gaukel, owner of the tavern that eventually became the Walper Hotel, used to keep a bear chained in his yard as a curiosity for his guests.

Public entertainment that featured larger, travelling attractions involving "wild" captive animals would have been almost unknown in rural areas of Upper Canada in the early 1800s and would have captured widespread interest. So, the announcement that a menagerie of wild beasts would exhibit in Galt on July 28, 1834, caused universal interest. For nearly twenty miles around, the coming exhibition was talked about. It became a topic of absorbing interest.

When the day arrived, there was, considering the circumstances, a large crowd, with people coming from Waterloo, Beverly, Woolwich, Blenheim, and other places more distant. It is estimated that there were about a thousand people at the three- hour performance. Inside the tent, sweltering heat made worse the already overwhelming stench and stagnant, suffocating air. No doubt, the attendees were forced to flee the tent in search of refreshment (including, most certainly, water) following the performance. And, let's face it, showmen have to eat, drink, and use the facilities to relieve themselves, too, right? Given the poor sanitary practices prevalent at the time, not to mention the fact that the food and water were likely contaminated with bacteria, it would be easy to transfer bacteria from one person to another.

Even before the entertainment, as has been mentioned, there were rumours that the company had brought the much-dreaded disease with them. According to James Young, "The report first arose from the illness of one of the showmen. He had been brought to the village a day or two before the menagerie arrived." Unfortunately, the rumours turned out to be true.

The man had appeared in Galt a day or so before the menagerie arrived, presumably to help set up. Locals had seen that he was ill and had asked the local doctor, Dr. Miller, to examine him. Dr. Miller's diagnosis was that the showman was suffering from Asiatic cholera. That had been enough to prompt the concerned locals to appear before Magistrate Shade on Monday, July 28, the day of the show, asking him to order cancellation. Shade, however, after some consideration, had declined.

Two days later, on Wednesday, upwards of thirty people presented with symptoms of cholera — and all of them had attended the show on Monday. More and more cases appeared on the Thursday and Friday, and a few new cases appeared over the several days after. The devastation of the disease was as widespread geographically as those who had travelled to view the show. The total death toll over the roughly ten-day period of the outbreak was nearly two hundred.

Death did not discriminate, claiming old as well as young. Families were now changed forever as they struggled to come to terms with their

Friedrich Gaukel c. 1850s.

losses. As the community struggled to rebuild itself, widows married widowers and combined their families and possessions. Orphaned children were often taken in by other families. Marriage became a survival strategy.

Bishop Benjamin Eby of Berlin lost his first wife, Mary, and eventually married Abraham Erb's widow, Magdalena. (Erb had died in 1830.) Friedrich Gaukel, a Berlin hotel keeper, lost his second wife, Maria Roschang, and their son, Heinrich. In nearby Blenheim Township, Moses Springer and his ten siblings were orphaned by the cholera epidemic. He was only ten years old at the time.

Some of the victims are recorded only by their first names or by the job that they did: "Milo, the hotel hosteler," or "Marshall, the cooper who attended the hotel dead." It is still sadder to say that even now there is no complete list of names or statistics that can account for all of the victims.[22]

The devastation caused by the disease is truly awe-inspiring. In Galt proper, a town of approximately two hundred, thirty-three people died in less than one week after the initial outbreak. The final death toll for the area was even worse. Of the one thousand attendees, there were, community-wide, at least two hundred deaths within the week. Putting that into perspective, the death toll for the surrounding region was equivalent to the erasure of the entire town of Galt.

The severity of the outbreak was made worse because, even though the village and area were developing in many respects, there was little to no infrastructure to care for the medical needs of all of those who fell ill. There was no hospital yet. One of the local churches was pressed into service as a makeshift infirmary and morgue. Dr. Miller was the sole physician at that time, though he was soon joined by a Dr. McQuarrie and Dr. John Scott, a recent twenty-one-year-old immigrant from Roxboroughshire, Scotland.

Writing of Scott, James Young observed, "Afterwards … [he] … became widely known in Berlin as a skilful practitioner and public-spirited citizen. Dr. Scott was one of the most fearless of the little band who fought the cholera inch by inch, with their lives in their hands, until it finally disappeared."

While it is true that the village population did rebuild itself in time, the personal losses would have been irrecoverable for those whose loved ones had perished.

Portrait of
Dr. John Scott.

One year after the outbreak (1835), it was discovered that there had been cholera-related deaths as close as twelve miles from the village — four days before the sick showman's arrival in Galt! That same year, Dr. Elim Stimson published a detailed pamphlet in Dundas, Ontario, on the 1834 cholera epidemic, inspired by his previous experience with the 1832 cholera outbreak in Montreal, when he had lost his own wife to the dreaded disease.

This was not the last cholera epidemic.[23] In 1851, for example, new immigrant Jacob Berndt died in Morriston (just outside of Galt) one week after his arrival there. Sadly, his three youngest children (of four) died, as well. Several years later, another citizen, Henry Becker, was remembered with a poignant obituary that noted he had arrived in Canada in 1854, "the year of the cholera."

The earlier victims who died in Galt are remembered, too. In local cemeteries weathered stone markers still keep watch. Bluntly, they reveal the sad truth: "Death by cholera, 1834."

3

THE UNDERGROUND RAILROAD MAKES A STOP IN WATERLOO COUNTY

> I was the conductor of the Underground Railroad for eight years, and I can say what most conductors can't say — I never ran my train off the track and I never lost a passenger.
>
> — Harriet Tubman (addressing a suffrage convention in New York, 1896)

THE PROBLEM WITH the ubiquitous Waterloo local history "story," as it has been told time and again (and as many of us have come to know it locally), is that white Pennsylvania Germans (many of whom were Mennonite) settled in the area as farmers, looking out for each other as a community and lending aid where it was needed. In other words, if someone needed a house or a barn built, then the whole community came out to build it. If someone's crops had failed, the community shared what it had and you would do the same, in kind. Until recently, the history of Waterloo focused almost entirely on these white settlers.

It is true that those early histories made some mention of the Indigenous Peoples who first occupied the area that later became Waterloo, but their presence was all but erased from the discussions of the periods that followed the arrival of Pennsylvania German settlers. Today, stories of the Indigenous Peoples who first occupied the land are finally also being told. Recently published books are helping to recuperate their histories.

What many don't know is that black settlers arrived in the Waterloo region at least as early as did the Mennonites. In fact, most residents of Waterloo Region are more than a little surprised to know that the area has a significant Canadian black history legacy.

Beginning in 1800, parties of Pennsylvania Germans arrived each year to settle upon the heavily forested but fertile lands of Waterloo County. Within those first few years, and as they began to clear the land and build their farms, black settlers, many of whom were fleeing the horrors of slavery, joined them in their search for freedom. Some found work on Mennonite farms as labourers, threshers, hostlers, and cowherds. As pacifists, the Mennonites were "passive abolitionists" regarding slavery, and so, rather than campaign openly against it, they quietly provided help and employment to those seeking asylum from it. A case could be made that this area's first refugees were arguably those fleeing for their lives from the bondage of slavery, arriving with little more than the clothes on their backs and their determination to build a better life.

One of the earliest stories concerns a young lad by the name of Isaac Jones. He was described by Waterloo County biographer Ezra Eby as "a colored boy brought to Canada by Abraham Erb [his employer]." Erb and his family arrived in Waterloo from Pennsylvania in 1806. Erb was a large landowner — his eventual land holdings were very large: over seven thousand acres. As a respected man, Erb was also well known for his community-building investments, which included the development of saw and grist mills, and the donation of land that was intended to be used for the construction of a school, a church, and a graveyard. (The school was built and became known locally as the 1820 log schoolhouse that is located today in Waterloo Park. This school is also tied to local black history and I will return to its story shortly.)

The 1820 log schoolhouse c. late 1890s, after it had been moved to its final resting place in Waterloo Park.

The mention of Isaac by Eby is significant for two reasons. First: Isaac is the first black person noted in the early history account of the area's first settlers. Second: Isaac was employed, not a slave, and was brought to Waterloo along with his employer's family, for whom he worked as a farm labourer. In effect, Isaac was the first black individual resident in Waterloo whose story has been told.

One particular incident from the life of Isaac bears particular attention. Apparently, young Isaac had been looking after some cattle in autumn when he (and they) got lost in the woods. These were early days in Waterloo, and the dense, old-growth forest no doubt impeded Isaac's efforts to find the cattle or his way home. His only companions were two dogs that remained by his side. To us, it might seem strange that the cattle were "loose," but at that time farm animals were mostly free-range. So, perhaps the cattle in question did wander deep into the woods to graze, and Isaac was trying to find them only after realizing how far they had actually gone.

When Isaac did not return with the cattle, he was missed. Ezra Eby tells us that "a great many went out to search for him" and that the search parties continued for more than a week. By that point, discouraged, most of them gave up in despair; but two men continued on with their search efforts. At some point, they heard the sound of dogs barking and came upon young Isaac, "almost dead from starvation and unable to walk." Ironically, their journey did not end there, as they realized that they also were now lost. They decided to cut through the brush in a straight direction and emerged on the Grand River just two miles south of the "little mill in Galt."

Eby says it was with great joy that they managed to get themselves and Isaac, "the object of their diligent search" back home safe and sound. The fact that the neighbouring community searched for him for over a week before he was found demonstrates how important he was to those who knew him.

Some years later, it seems, Isaac was still in close contact with Erb. A land "sale" transaction for 224 acres (lot 102 German Company Tract) was registered between Abraham Erb to one Isaac Jones, dated May 20, 1819 (one year before the construction of the log schoolhouse). On May 11, 1822, Jones sold all 224 acres of lot 102 to Christian Hoffman, a Wesleyan Methodist farmer from Pennsylvania. A question remains: were the 224 acres a gift from Erb to Jones to be used as a nest egg, or had Jones been able to save enough money over the years to buy the land from Erb? We may never know, but it is interesting to note that Jones chose to sell the entire 224 acres only a few years after acquiring it. This sale would have afforded him a tidy sum with which to build a good life.

Slavery was officially outlawed in Canada in the 1830s. I say "officially" since, unofficially, there were ways around the legislation, and slaves could still be hunted down and returned to their owners — often for a hefty reward. In the United States, many states, especially those in the South, continued to practise slavery up until the end of the Civil War.

As the anti-slavery movement gained political support on both sides of the Canada–U.S. border, some very brave individuals were taking action against slavery — risking everything to help those who searched for freedom. The Underground Railroad had been firmly established, and abolitionists (those who opposed slavery), both black and white, helped fugitive slaves. Most of the black activists were free, but some were slaves themselves.

The nineteenth-century "Underground Railroad" was obviously neither underground nor a rail line. Rather, it was a well-connected secret network of escape routes, many of which led to Canada. It has been estimated that, by 1850, as many as a hundred thousand slaves may have found freedom because of the Underground Railroad's brave "conductors." (Using railroad terminology, the abolitionists associated with this complex escape route referred to themselves as "conductors.")

Some researchers have suggested that the network was active as early as 1780, and continued to run into the early part of the U.S. Civil War (roughly 1860 to 1862). However, it is generally accepted that it was at its height from the 1850s. The need for the Underground Railroad ended when Abraham Lincoln issued the Emancipation Proclamation in 1863, which effectively freed all slaves.

One man who helped the fugitive slaves was William Still. He was just a boy when he assisted in the escape of his first slave. He never knew the man's name, only that he was being hunted by slave-catchers. In the years after, he would help hundreds more. Not only did Still help fugitive slaves escape those bent on capturing them, he also went to extraordinary lengths to record the names and stories of those he helped. He vowed that their stories would never be forgotten. As there are virtually no records for many of those who were slaves — they were only ever listed in slave owners' account books as chattels and property — Still's records are invaluable to the many descendants of slaves who today are researching their ancestry.

In his book, *The Underground Railroad*, Still kept meticulous but secret records of the many escapees who passed through the Philadelphia "station" where he worked. All told, in his fourteen years of work with the "railroad" he personally helped over eight hundred to escape to freedom in Canada (particularly southern Ontario). After the Civil War, Still published the secret notes he'd kept in diaries during those years. His book contains some of the best evidence we have of the workings of the Underground Railroad, detailing the seekers who used it, including where they came from, how they escaped, and the families they left behind.

FIRST BLACK CANADIAN SETTLEMENT IN WATERLOO COUNTY

Paola Brown was one ex-slave who credited his freedom to the efforts of the Underground Railroad network. Eventually he made his way to Hamilton, where he became a leader and activist among his people. In 1828, dreaming of independent land ownership, Brown and his followers petitioned the government to create a land company (with Paola as their agent) so they could establish a black community of their own in the Clergy Reserves along the Grand River. Their petition (and a subsequent request) were denied summarily; they were told that the land, although surveyed, was not for sale (at least not to them). Although they were aware of another black settlement in Oro Township, they felt this was too far away, and so they continued searching for suitable land upon which they could settle. In 1832, and undeterred by previous setbacks, Paola and thirty-four people (nine households) decided to settle in Woolwich Township in an area known as Crook's Tract (which was located near modern-day Winterbourne). They named their settlement "Colbornesburg" (in honour of Lieutenant-Governor John Colborne) and eventually established a church and a school.

Although they were proud of their efforts, life was unbelievably hard and failure loomed at every turn. The land Paola and his people had settled on had been surveyed, but it was wild and untamed. It teemed with wildlife and other resources such as excellent water and fertile land, but in its natural state it could not sustain an agricultural community. The party tried their best to clear the land and make it into viable farmland; however, it turned out that many lacked the necessary tools to till the land. To make matters worse, many were not accustomed to the harsh Canadian weather, particularly the winter months, and did not know how to ensure that their food supplies would last until the following year's harvest. To survive, many ended up turning to others for help, but their reliance on their neighbours for survival ultimately strained everyone's resolve.

THE QUEEN'S BUSH SETTLEMENT

By 1837 almost everybody had left the little settlement. Paola moved back to Hamilton, where he continued to engage his fellow ex-slaves with public, politically charged speeches and to lobby the government for the same things their white neighbours already took for granted — like the right to land ownership.

Some of the Colbornesburg settlers chose to stay closer to home. Some moved northeast of Waterloo, settling in Conestoga, while the majority settled along the boundary between Peel Township (Wellington County) and Wellesley Township (Waterloo County). This area was known as the Queen's Bush, a largely unsettled area that ran from Waterloo and Wellington counties, west to Lake Huron and south to Amherstberg (another area with a strong Canadian black history legacy). The area was relatively isolated from established roads. It was said that a trip from Hawkesville to Waterloo was a two-day affair — one day into Waterloo through the forest to civilization and one day back through and deeper into the bush. Today, Hawkesville is about a ten-minute drive from Waterloo. Glen Alan, Wallenstein, and Yatton were even further inland.

In 1837, however, because the area was still isolated, no one appeared to be too bothered if someone lacking proper ownership rights decided to set up a home there. Most of this group settled illegally at first, as squatters, because the land they had settled on was waiting to be surveyed by the government and put up for sale. The majority of the squatters hoped that, with hard work, in a year or two they would be able to save enough to be able to purchase their land outright. Little did they know that they would wait thirteen years before the government agreed to sell them the land. In the meantime they continued to lobby the government for the rights to purchase the lands they had settled upon, worked, and developed over time.

No strangers to adversity, the settlers had the hard work of trying to clear what was, like Colbornesburg, untamed timberland. Although the area had abundant wild game and streams full of fish, the land was covered with dense forest. The soil was rich, perfect for agriculture, but the settlers had to face the nasty and exhausting business of clearing it. They persevered, however, and cleared the land in order to cultivate it — an act of survival, really. In doing so, however, they were setting a kind of trap for themselves, creating a bit of a Catch-22. While they were petitioning the government to sell the land to them, they were helping to make sure that they wouldn't be able to afford it if it did become available. By working (and developing) the land they did not own, they were actually driving up its value and, sadly, putting it beyond what they could afford. When the government finally agreed to sell the lots, most could not afford to buy them.

Before that fateful day, though, a small community emerged, and by 1841 the black settlers had established a church of their own in Peel Township (the African Methodist Episcopal Church). Its first preacher was an African-American from South Carolina named Morris Brown. Over the years, the church served a dwindling membership, until the last services were held there in 1918 and the building was demolished.

For those who settled here, life was back-breaking and tenuous. Few were able to prosper in the early years. Many, as mentioned earlier, in addition to lacking tools and finances, were also finding the harsh Canadian winters to be particularly difficult. Starvation was a very real threat, especially during long winter months when there were no crops. Some were given help and support from their Mennonite neighbours, like merchant Henry Sauder Huber, who was himself the son of a Pennsylvania pioneer. These Mennonites provided newcomers with seed for planting and household goods, and also lent them tools to break and clear the land.

Despite all of the difficulties the settlers faced, there were success stories. One couple, John and Eliza Little, who arrived in the Queen's Bush area in February of 1841 eventually became among the area's most prosperous landowners. At one point, they owned several hundred acres of profitable farmland. Although he found success eventually, John Little had a hard early life — one that, unfortunately, was not unique to him. As a slave, he had consistently defied his "owners" and often received brutal beatings as punishment for his rebellion. After he had escaped several times, his owners gave up on him, feeling he was too much trouble. To make whatever further money they could off him, they sold him.

His new owner also owned Little's future wife, Eliza. Eliza had been separated from her parents as a child and grew up working as a domestic servant. She, too, had received frequent beatings. When she was sixteen she married John Little, at which point her master assigned her to work in the fields alongside him. The work was back-breaking and almost destroyed her will. Following an almost insurmountable series of hardships, the Littles managed to escape and reached Chicago, where some kind abolitionists paid for their journey to Canada. They finally crossed over the border at Windsor.

Unable to find work in the Windsor area, they travelled to Hamilton, where they purchased two axes — one for each of them — half a dozen plates, knives, forks, an iron pot, one Dutch oven, and some food: a fifty-pound bag of flour and twenty pounds of pork. They headed for a community they had heard about in the Wellesley area and eventually came to the Queen's Bush, where, over time, they managed to build up their resources and became prosperous.

Describing their arrival at what would otherwise have been, perhaps, the worst of times, John's words reflected the couple's determination to succeed: "We marched right into the wilderness where there were thousands of acres of woods which the chain never run round since Adam. At night, we built a fire, and cut down a tree, and put up some slats like a wigwam. This was in February when the snow was two feet deep."

It is interesting to note that some years later, following the end of the Civil War in the States, there was a migration of ex-slaves from Canada to Haiti, which was being touted as an opportunity for hope and new beginnings. Many, including the Littles, left Canada and journeyed, yet again, to lands far away and toward an uncertain future. It is not known what happened to the Littles, but we do know that the settlement opportunities in Haiti were not exactly as promised.

In the years following the arrival of the Littles, the Queen's Bush Settlement — in a modest fashion — grew and prospered. As it did so, the institutions associated with a prospering community began to appear. As mentioned, a church was established in the community; so, too, eventually, was a school.

Many of the adult black settlers in the Queen's Bush Settlement were illiterate, having known only the brutal life of a slave working outside in the fields and blistering sun on southern plantations. In many areas, particularly in the southern States, it was illegal to teach a slave to read and write. Literacy was a dream for many who had been denied it, and so parents, coming to freedom in Canada, were eager for their children to have the opportunities they did not have. In 1844, after the community established a school in the Wellesley area (the Mount Pleasant Mission School), a teacher arrived. She happened to be white. Her name was Fidelia Cobourn, and she was an abolitionist missionary from Maine.

The school relied on donations — many of which came from other abolitionists in the United States. Sadly, but not unexpectedly, these donations were, at times, rather sparse. Fidelia could not afford to secure independent lodgings for herself, so she moved into the school she helped to establish. Existence was tenuous. One year after her arrival, in 1845, a drought destroyed much of the community's crops. Fidelia noticed that some of her students were arriving at school so hungry that they ate the food scraps that she had set aside to feed her milk cow. Obtaining sufficient funding to run the school and pay her salary became a constant and abiding battle. In many ways it was a losing one. Despite the community's collective efforts, including Fidelia's campaigns for donations, the proverbial writing was on the wall. The choice for many in the community was difficult but became increasingly clear: do we stay and perhaps starve, or should we leave and start again somewhere else?

Consider this: In 1848, there were about 1,500 blacks living in the Queen's Bush area of Waterloo-Wellington counties. By 1851 there were only 237 recorded in the census. By comparison, there were approximately 700 people in total living in Berlin (Kitchener) at that time, and Berlin, as an urban centre, was economically booming. As school enrolment continued to dwindle in the Queen's Bush, the last black school closed its doors for good in 1853. The remaining children were integrated into common schools in the surrounding areas. Some of the black settlers went back to the States in search of family members they had left behind. Others moved on to the Chatham and Windsor areas. Some came to Berlin.

PETER EDWARD SUSAND

One of these was a man I find particularly interesting. Peter Edward Susand, born in 1803, was a former slave from New Orleans who escaped to Oakville, Upper Canada, in 1837. By 1843 he and his wife were farming a fifty-acre farm in Wellesley Township on lot 1, concession 12. It is not known if he owned or rented it.

Peter's wife, Elizabeth Liticott, had been born in England. She was white. There were at least five biracial marriages in the area at that time.

Peter Edward Susand's barber shop (third building from left) c. 1850s.

Peter and Elizabeth had ten children, and sometime between 1851 and 1853 he and his family relocated to Berlin, where he became an established member of the community. He was ambitious and had a strong business sense, having established enterprises: he was the first barber in the town of Berlin, and at some point he opened the Meridian Coffee Salon (some accounts say "Saloon").

He was a unique man, with a love of literature and particularly Shakespeare. Peter even named some of his children after characters in Shakespeare's plays, including a son named Othello Leopold. Susand had taken a leadership role in the Queen's Bush community and had a reputation as a polished orator of powerful, moving speeches. In 1856 the *Berlin News* dated April 9 referred to a public political debate in which Susand was known as "the first colored gentleman who practised the tonsorial art in Berlin." It is clear that he had some formal education. At some point he composed and self-published poems, entitled *The Prose and Poetical Works of Peter Edward Susand*. Unfortunately, only two lines of his work seem to have survived, but they indicate a wry sense of humour:

> *"Ye ho! Here comes a schooner!*
> *Eh ho! I wish she'd come a little sooner."*

Susand was also very protective of his business interests. Sometime between 1853 and1857, he initiated and won several legal proceedings against some whites who had damaged his Berlin property. In the first case, Susand received five shillings from one of the hooligans (Jacob Brieler) as payment for damages. One of the justices of the peace in the case was none other than magistrate Henry Sauder Huber, who, as previously mentioned, had provided help for some of the black settlers in the Queen's Bush area in their early struggles.

Susand's learning and skill as an orator were of great use when, in 1856, he embarked on a political career. In that year he was nominated for Berlin town councillor. He was delighted and addressed the assembly upon his nomination. His speech was most eloquent. Unfortunately, he did not stand much of a chance since he was running against incumbent Dr. John Scott, who had been in the position for a number of years after having made a name for himself as one of the cholera doctors in the 1834 Galt epidemic. Susand lost the election to Dr. Scott; however, Scott did not hold office for long, dying later that same year of consumption. In 1857 the position was filled by another well-known white man … Henry Sauder Huber.

Peter and Elizabeth Susand lost several children during the early 1850s, and there is speculation that this weighed heavily enough upon them that they chose to baptize all of their remaining children at one time, on April 13, 1862. The Susand family were registered members of one of the earliest churches in this area: St. John the Evangelist, Anglican (located on Water Street in Kitchener). The Susands were continuing to reinvent themselves with new business ventures and had proven to be contributing members of their community.

At some point after the baptism, Peter departed for Guelph, leaving his family to fend for themselves. The assumption of researcher Linda Brown-Kubisch is that the family had been abandoned. They fell on hard times following his departure. Elizabeth Susand eventually established her own successful business selling confectionaries. Her children would help her and would sometimes sell her wares at the Berlin train station. Her business, known simply as Susand's Taffy, became very successful, and its proceeds enabled her to eventually purchase her own property. By 1865 Elizabeth referred to herself as a widow, but it is not clear if Peter was, in fact, dead, or if, although he was still alive, Elizabeth chose to change her status because she considered the rift in the marriage permanent.

Sometime after this, Elizabeth's sons moved to Michigan and eventually sent for their mother to join them. The family members that stayed in Berlin were buried in Mount Hope Cemetery in Kitchener.

THE WELLINGTON INSTITUTE

Peter Susand may have been Berlin's first barber, but he was not the only black man to open or operate a business in Waterloo County. In December 1840 a new secondary school opened at the rear of the Royal Exchange Hotel, which was located in the east end of Berlin. The Wellington Institute was a private school that charged a "moderate rate" of tuition to its students (two dollars per student, plus a personal allotment for heating fuel for the classroom).

Its schoolmaster, John Frederick Augustus Sykes Fayette, described by his Berlin neighbours as being a "well-educated mulatto man," was the first in the area to offer formalized instruction in English grammar and, presumably, geography, as he was also credited as being the first to make use of a map in his classroom. Fayette had graduated from Case Western Reserve University in 1836 — the first African-American to graduate from that institution. He spent the next year in Hudson, Ohio, as a theology student. In 1837, several years prior to his opening of the Wellington Institute in Berlin, an early marriage record lists Fayette as being married to Emily Preston, a white woman. Around 1840, Fayette was working as a missionary and travelling throughout southern Ontario when he and Emily chose to settle in Waterloo County and open a school.

Education was an important value for the citizens of Waterloo County (for both boys and girls). Public schools were established early in the area's settlement years. Thomas Pearce, veteran school inspector for Waterloo County, provided an historical overview of early education in the 1914 Waterloo Historical Society Annual Volume:

> That desire to have their children receive a good, practical education, which is a marked characteristic of the

> inhabitants of this county today, manifested itself just as strongly in the pioneers in the early part of the last century. Prior to 1842 all schools were voluntary. They were kept in private houses, meeting houses, abandoned dwellings, unused shops or under any available and convenient shelter. On in the 20's and 30's an occasional small log schoolhouse was built and paid for by private subscription. Schools were kept open during the winter months only. The teachers were mostly itinerants — ex-soldiers or unsuccessful tradesmen — who were engaged in other occupations the rest of the year. Their scholarship was unknown, examinations and certificates being unheard of. [Underlining as in the original.]

Reverend Fayette's education gave him far better qualifications than those of other teachers in the area. Fayette was a university graduate at a time when most people ended school around the Grade 8 level. It was unusual that a man with his education would come to Waterloo County to serve as a teacher; it was even more unusual that a highly educated and ambitious black man — a man who had not been a slave — would come to Waterloo County of his own volition. It seems, though, that Waterloo County's residents did not find Fayette's race to be an issue; rather, they considered themselves lucky, indeed.

Although many of Berlin's merchant class could afford the fees for the school, there were those of average means who could not. Fayette's school was underfunded, and eventually he ran out of money and went into debt. The school closed and Fayette left the area (and, apparently, his unpaid creditors) behind. Fayette made his way to the Hamilton area, where he served for some years (1845 to 1850) as the minister for the Barton Stone United Church, After serving as the minister in Barton, Reverend Fayette spent time as an Ontario school superintendent before retiring to London, where he died in 1876.

In Waterloo County, Reverend Fayette's legacy is an important one. A free man, Fayette showed that there was hope for other blacks who, at the time, were struggling for freedom from slavery. As a black university

Israel D. Bowman, graduate of the Wellington Institute, before his death in 1896, age 66.

graduate, he served as a role model for his contemporaries (and for future generations) in the black community, And as the first black teacher in Waterloo County and founder of an institute of higher learning, he provided education that helped the lives of those he taught.

Two of his students, no doubt the better for having attended the Wellington Institute, matured and made their own contributions to the area's history. Jacob Yost Shantz attended the Wellington Institute when he was eighteen years old and eventually became a successful businessman, a mayor of Berlin, and an avid supporter of Mennonite resettlement from Russia to Manitoba in the latter part of the nineteenth century. Schantz was also locally known for his herbal medicines and cancer treatments. Another student at the Institute, Israel David Bowman, attended the school at the tender age of eleven. Bowman's later accomplishments included becoming the reeve for the village of Berlin in 1858 and county clerk in 1861. It is in this capacity that Bowman is arguably best known.

ROBERT SUTHERLAND

Robert Sutherland was, like Reverend Fayette, a free man and an educated man. Born in Jamaica in 1830, Sutherland was the son of an African-Jamaican woman and a Scottish father. His father, a white naval officer of some financial means, left money for Robert's education. Leaving Jamaica, Sutherland came to Canada and enrolled in Queen's College, Kingston (today known as Queen's University).

The college had opened in 1842, having been granted a charter one year earlier. It is not known why Sutherland chose to attend Queen's or, for that matter, why he chose to move to British North America to advance his education. Queen's College had been founded to provide training to men interested in becoming Presbyterian clergy (as a Scot, his father may have been Presbyterian).

Regardless, Robert Sutherland enrolled at Queen's in 1847. He was the first man of African descent to attend the college as an undergraduate — a feat in and of itself. A popular and well-liked student, he was diligent and dedicated, excelling in all of his studies, particularly the art of debate. During his three-year undergraduate career, he won fourteen academic prizes, including one in Latin that was awarded to him by his fellow students.

Sutherland graduated in 1852 with double honours in mathematics and classics. Upon graduation, he enrolled as a law student at Osgoode Hall in Toronto and was called to the bar in 1855. Credited with being the first black person to become a member of the Law Society of Upper Canada, Sutherland became the first black lawyer to practise in Canada. Later that year, Robert moved to Berlin, where he devoted some of his practice to helping ex-slaves in the Queen's Bush to gain title to the lands that they had petitioned the government to sell to them.

There is a story about Mr. Sutherland that, in my opinion, shows how respected he was in this community and how highly his fellow citizens thought of him. During the time that Henry Sauder Huber (yes, him again!) was the mayor of Berlin, a travelling circus came to Berlin. Huber was in office from 1857 to 1859. This circus is not to be confused with the travelling menagerie that visited Galt in 1834. Circuses, like menageries, had captive animals that performed tricks for the audiences, but circuses also had human performers, including clowns.

Sutherland had purchased a ticket to attend and was sitting with the rest of the crowd. During the show, he was subjected to racist heckling by a clown, who singled him out. Apparently, a half a dozen or so of Sutherland's neighbouring guests, angry on his behalf, rose up out of their seats and gave chase to the clown, who ran away and disappeared into the nearby woods in a vain attempt to hide. Mayor Huber later released a statement about the affair to the local newspaper, stating that the citizens of Berlin would of course sympathize with their "coloured" neighbour, as many of them were Mennonites who were not in support of slavery (or, apparently, of racism).

The circus was driven out of town, but what of the clown? It was discovered that he was in fact the owner of the circus, Dan Rice, who often performed in his own show. The Rice Circus was a particularly successful and famous circus troupe during the mid- to late-nineteenth century and was eventually bought out by one of its early employees and showmen: none other than P.T. Barnum!

And as for Robert Sutherland? He eventually left Berlin and moved his practice north to Walkerton, where he enjoyed a successful law career, even serving briefly as reeve of the town. Upon his untimely death from pneumonia in 1878, following a business trip to Toronto, Mr. Sutherland, who had never married, bequeathed his entire net worth (approximately $13,000) to Queen's University, making him Queen's first major benefactor. Sutherland was credited posthumously as the "black man who saved Queen's University," since the money he endowed the university with enabled it to weather a very difficult financial period. According to lawyer and author Anthony Morgan, the $13,000 that Sutherland gave would, in today's dollars, be worth somewhere in the neighbourhood of over $260,000. Sutherland's legacy lives on at Queen's, where there are scholarships in his name. In March 1998 a building, Sutherland Hall, was named after him and dedicated in his memory.

LEVI CARROLL

Some cultures are excellent record-keepers, whereas others — not so much. In the case of black history, especially slave history, records have been notoriously difficult to track down. More often than not, only one name may exist for a slave in a ledger book of accounts — a first name or nickname. Perhaps, as it was common enough practice then, the slave may have the owner's last name and be listed as "chattel" that may be sold or transferred upon the death of the owner to his heirs. For African slaves, many names were changed (or "Christianized," as the process was known to slave traders or owners) once they were sold, whereby their original African tribal names disappeared. Records regarding black slaves, then, until regular census-taking began in the mid-1800s, were more individualized and usually found in bills of sale or transfer, wills, ledgers, etc. Sometimes, however, other means of gathering information can be quite fruitful, if unconventional: legal interactions — e.g., arrests for runaways, etc. — were often reported in the newspapers of the time. Church records can also be of use. It just depends.

A now iconic photo taken by an unknown photographer sometime after 1874, when Berlin High School was built (today it is known as KCI or Kitchener Collegiate Institute), and before 1893–94, when the log house was moved to Waterloo Park. Berlin High School towers in the distance behind the former log schoolhouse. Levi Carroll and his family sit in front of the house.

When I first encountered the name Levi Carroll, I was engaged in what I thought was unrelated research. I was working on a project to trace the history and provenance of the "1820 log schoolhouse" that is located (today) in Waterloo Park. I knew when I began my research that its current location was not its first, but as I followed the information before me, a larger story was revealed. For one thing, the log schoolhouse wasn't always just a school. For more years than it was a schoolhouse, it was also a residence. A home.

Levi Carroll was a former slave from Maryland who lived for an extended period of time — nearly fifty years, to be exact — in the 1820 log schoolhouse after it had been repurposed from being a school. The school had been built by Pennsylvania German Mennonites on land donated by Abraham Erb (see Isaac Jones's story, above). It was in continual use until 1842, when class enrolment surpassed the capacity of the small log building. It was dismantled and moved to its second location in Berlin/Kitchener (today that would be adjacent to Kitchener Collegiate Institute or KCI). It was at some point after the schoolhouse's move in 1842 that Levi Carroll rented it as his new home.

Levi Carroll first shows up in the 1851 census for Berlin. The listing shows Levi Carroll, his wife, and a son, Charlie. Levi worked for one of the early Mennonite settlers, Abraham Weber, who came to Waterloo County from Pennsylvania in 1807. While working for Weber, Levi incurred an injury the exact details of which are not clear, but author William Uttley mentions in *A History of Kitchener* that Levi's injury could have been a broken arm or leg. In the only known photograph of Levi (see previous page), he is sitting outside the schoolhouse and it is clear that he is missing his right leg below the knee. Could this have been the injury Uttley mentions? We do not know for sure. However, following Levi's accident, Abraham Weber gave him some land for a "cabin and a garden," according to Uttley. Clearly, Weber felt strongly enough about Levi's service to him (and about his personal welfare) to help him to provide for his family's food and shelter. No doubt the cabin was the log schoolhouse that had been relocated from Waterloo to Berlin in 1842. Whether or not Levi owned the land on which it was located is not certain, but records show that he was paying $5 per month rent to a landlord, about which he complained bitterly, feeling the sum to be exorbitant. (Incidentally, Levi's landlord was John Hoffman, who was the only man in Waterloo Region history to ever be mayor/reeve of both Berlin and/or Waterloo).

By working for Weber, and later for others, Levi contributed to the local economy and his community. Over the years, Levi's occupation is mentioned in census records, but it appears that he did not remain in only one role. Several of the censuses refer to him as a labourer. One says he was a tile worker and another says he was a gardener. No doubt he was all of these. And perhaps, like many today, he changed jobs frequently to "get by" as best as he could. Some of the written accounts seem to make a point of noting that Levi raised vegetables in his garden, referring specifically to potatoes and corn. One may wonder why this would even be of any interest to anyone, but apparently Levi did not work the garden in the usual ways. Stories indicate that his neighbours would come to watch him work because his method of doing so hearkened back to the southern plantations — he worked his garden with a long-handled hoe under one arm, which was not the local technique. It made him something of a neighbourhood curiosity.

Perhaps the oddest thing about Levi was that he was literate. As previously mentioned, it had been illegal in many Southern places to teach a slave to read. In each of the census records, Levi and each of his children are listed as being able to read. Levi's son Charles, aged sixteen in 1851, went to school in Berlin, and is listed as the only black child in attendance. At that time it was called Central School, although today locals would be more familiar with its current name, Suddaby Public School.

Levi lived a long life and was in his late nineties at the time of his death. He was married at least three times and outlived each of his wives. Incidentally, each of those wives either came from or had strong ties to the Queen's Bush Settlement in the Wellesley area. Levi's first known marriage, which was to Creasia (Lucretia) Brooks, took place in Berlin on February 22, 1846, which was four years after the log schoolhouse had moved to where Levi was to live for the next forty years or more. At the time of their marriage, Levi, at thirty, was listed as twenty years younger than his new wife. Since the school records show their son Charles was sixteen in 1851, he would have been born about 1835. If the numbers and ages recorded are all correct, it Charles may not have been Levi's biological son. Although there are no records, Creasia probably passed away somewhere between 1852 and 1854, because Levi married again.

Levi's second wife was Anna Emile Timlet. According to their marriage certificate, she and Levi were married on December 17, 1854. There are no children mentioned in connection with this marriage in the census records, but it appears that Anna died sometime in 1860. Levi's third wife was Margaret Moore Johnston, who was from the Queen's Bush. Margaret had one daughter, Emiline, who was already six or seven years old when Margaret married Levi on October 2, 1861. A birth of a son, John Carroll, is registered in 1865. Some years later, in 1884, Emiline Johnston Carroll, then aged twenty-nine or thirty, married James Aylestock (from Elmira, a barber) and they had a son, William James Aylestock (born in 1886). Emiline's husband, James, seems to have disappeared from subsequent census records. Emiline returned with their son, William, to live with Margaret and Levi in the small log house.

Margaret died on February 19, 1890, and Levi's life changed significantly. According to one of his obituaries, Levi "fell on hard times" after Margaret's death and was forced to enter the Waterloo County House of Industry and Refuge (along with Emiline and William) in 1891. The schoolhouse remained vacant until 1894, when the town of Waterloo purchased it and moved it to its present location in Waterloo Park.

Levi eventually died on July 15, 1897, in the House of Industry. Several sources claimed that he was nearly one hundred years old at the time of his death. What I found most poignant was that there were two obituaries published about his life. They were posted several days apart and, surprisingly, written by different people. One may well ponder why an obscure, disabled, literate, ex-slave was remembered by his neighbours and friends in death — not once, but twice. In fact, they remembered him fondly, speaking of him as "a man whom almost every citizen knows." That his obituary was posted twice and commented on by a former neighbour who clearly respected him tells me that Levi may not have been a wealthy man, but, having outlived many who were, was indeed a man who was well regarded by his peers and neighbours. In terms of community and a legacy, who could ask for more?

Emiline was infirm and spent the rest of her life, too, in the House of Industry. She died of heart failure on February 17, 1943. William Aylestock

The Lawson family home in Glen Allen c. 1920s.

left the House of Industry as a young man at about age sixteen. From there, he went to Brooklyn, New York, and stayed with relatives before eventually returning to live with family still living in the Queen's Bush area. William met and married a woman by the name of Jemima (Minnie) Lawson.

The Lawson family had deep roots in the Wellesley area and were one of the first families to establish themselves in the Queen's Bush. William and Minnie had a happy marriage that was blessed with eight children. Their eldest child was Addie Aylestock, the first woman ordained in the British Episcopal Church in Canada (and the first African-Canadian woman to be ordained in Canada). Her sister, Rella Braithwaite, became an accomplished writer and researcher of Canadian black history who aided the Ontario Ministry of Education to develop a black studies guide for use in the classroom. Her daughter, Diana Braithwaite, is a well-known jazz and blues artist, whose music and performances incorporate the stories of her ancestral roots in the Underground Railroad. Addie and Rella's brother Lloyd was an engineer and the first black man to be hired at the Avro Aircraft plant in Toronto (1938). Brother Frank taught electronics following his service in the Second World War. Minnie was particularly remembered by her family's Mennonite friends as a wonderful cook whose pies were famous, feeding many a hungry farm labourer and neighbour from miles around.

When we deal with history, it is important to remember that our local early settlement story is a multicultural one that includes refugees coming to Canada with the best of intentions for a better future, full of hope, doing their best to "fit in" and "get by" in spite of their lack of privilege or even the simplest of amenities. For the black settlers of Waterloo County, many of whom were ex-slaves, their journey to freedom in Canada was made easier when others stepped in to help. At other times the journey was difficult and they forged ahead alone, but determined to succeed. Their stories are a legacy that continues to amaze and educate, if only we will listen.

PART TWO

Containment

4

MISFITS, MISCHIEF, AND MISFORTUNE: FITTING IN OR FALLING OUT

> And those that were seen dancing were thought to be insane by those who could not hear the music.
>
> — Friedrich Nietzsche

CANADA IS PROUD of its international reputation as a peacekeeper. Domestically, its motto is "peace, order, and good government." There is an expectation that vulnerable citizens will be looked after and that those who hurt others (physically, emotionally, or economically) will face penalties in the name of the greater social good. This idealized picture of how things work does not represent the everyday reality for everyone, however.

For example, the Truth and Reconciliation Commission, created to examine the historical injustices suffered by the Indigenous Peoples in Canada, has revealed in the starkest ways possible the gross mistreatment that governing agencies, and those acting on behalf of them, have inflicted. Further, the commission has shown that this mistreatment is not just a thing of the past. In fact, the situation remains dire. Indigenous women, for example, are overrepresented in prison populations. Suicide ranks as a leading cause of death among young people on reserves. Reserve schools are seriously underfunded, and many Indigenous youth do not graduate from high school, let alone attend university.

In the larger Canadian population, there are also funding gaps. The current premier of Ontario has said that the province is "open for business," while at the same time claiming that he has a "Plan for the People." The two claims seem to be at odds. Indeed, if one looks at the government's decision to freeze the minimum wage, roll back holiday and health benefits for part-time workers, and remove the cap on rents, it becomes very clear which group is really benefiting from the "Plan for the People." In Ontario, there are current budget cuts for important education programs, emergency medical services, medical staffing, and accessible social housing. Many of these social programs, which were intended to provide help and assistance to various at-risk individuals and families in need, are now nonexistent or seriously underfunded. In other words, those most vulnerable are getting left behind by the current version of the system that was supposed to help them.

Was it always like this? Let's step back in time for a bit of context. Social welfare was once called "charity."

In medieval Britain, charity was generally considered to be the responsibility of the nobles. They gave tiny fractions of their wealth to help the poor and the sick. The social expectation was that to be part of "the nobility," those with titles and land and wealth, one also had to have "nobility," i.e., one had the moral responsibility to help those less fortunate. The term for this practice was *noblesse oblige* (to be a noble you needed to act nobly). Alms were given out at churches, and, sometimes, food and clothing were dispensed at monasteries and estates. Beggars (also called mendicants) roamed the countryside looking for relief.

But since there was no law about it, nothing specified how generous a donor was required to be. A couple of stale loaves of bread thrown into the street in the general direction of a starving beggar could be seen to be charity. Throughout the Middle Ages and into the Reformation era, more pressure was put on churches to provide charity within their parish jurisdictions. The local churches — which would have originally been Catholic but, after the Reformation in the early 1500s, likely would have been Anglican in

England or Presbyterian in Scotland — were the ones who controlled, governed, and yes, doled out any charity to those they deemed worthy of such. The first asylum created in England to deal with madness was "Bedlam," originating in 1247 from the Priory of the New Order of Our Lady of Bethlehem. It was originally established as a centre to collect alms for distribution but evolved into a specialized institution for the insane.

During the reign of Elizabeth I, things changed somewhat with the institution of the 1601 Poor Law. This legislation was instituted to quantify and qualify the processes for deciding if potential recipients were eligible (or worthy) to receive any care or assistance from the government. For those lucky enough to be deemed worthy of care, the law stipulated how that assistance was to be delivered and how much aid would be given. In some ways it was a step forward, but it also reinforced the notions of the *deserving poor* and the *undeserving poor.* It was during this time that a new institution was created: the work house, where inmates were expected to earn their keep.

Although the situation is much altered now, judgments regarding "worthiness" continue to persist in society today. Those who are poor, differently abled, or addicted are sometimes still stigmatized. It has been said that a society should be judged by the way that it treats its most vulnerable citizens. If that's the case, it must be admitted that contemporary society is still wanting.

In the early days in Waterloo County, social assistance and aid offered for those mentally or physically challenged was very much determined by the concepts of the deserving and undeserving poor.

As the general population grew, particularly in urban areas, life became more complex and traditional social supports became strained. Where families once provided for their aged, mentally ill, or disabled relatives, many people were now working outside the home (perhaps within one of the numerous factories) to just feed themselves. As a result, they were not available to help their needy family members.

This was recognized by the government, which began to be more involved in society's regulation. The government's response to poverty and the need for assistance was largely regulatory, but money was given to local communities to help them deal with those in their area who could not care for themselves, such as the mentally ill, the disabled, and orphaned and neglected children. But, even after Confederation, the provision of social welfare continued to be irregular and piecemeal, often influenced by the philanthropic concerns of the upper class — in particular those women who viewed charitable activities as an extension of their maternal roles and as an acceptable undertaking in society. Those who campaigned for temperance, suffrage, prison reform, etc., were largely women from the upper class. More often than not, they were the wives of industrialists.

The first extensive debate in Canada to deal with child welfare was in Toronto. This occurred in the late 1880s and eventually led to the founding of the Toronto Children's Aid Society in 1891. The first society for the prevention of the cruelty to animals was created in England in 1824. It originally called for provisions for children as well, but its main concern was provision for the care of abandoned and abused animals. The first Humane Society in Canada was established in Montreal in 1869, followed by one in Toronto in 1873. Separate legislation for children's welfare didn't happen until many years later. Children were often measured by the same moral yardstick as adults, both legally and socially. They could be incarcerated along with adults, and many roamed in groups as beggars, sometimes becoming involved in crime just to survive.

Disability and mental health was another matter. During the nineteenth century, individuals with mental health problems, physical disabilities, or mental disabilities were often placed in jail or in institutions, as their families were unable or unwilling to care for them. Among the general population, there was often little distinction made between those who had committed crimes and those with mental or physical health issues. Waterloo County had no institution specifically designed to care for the mentally ill and did not have a hospital until the 1890s. Some locals deemed mentally ill were housed in the county jail or the poorhouse, while others were transferred to the closest facility that would take them. In the case of Waterloo, that was usually the Hamilton Insane Asylum, which had originally been intended to be a hospital for the accommodation and treatment of alcoholics.

There were many reasons why many could not cope with their own problems or those of others: family breakdown, death of a caregiver, situational poverty, etc. Some patients became lost in the system that was supposed to care for them while others eventually were able to return to their families.

Others were not so fortunate and suffered great abuse and despair while in institutional care and imposed confinement. Here are some of their stories.

5

THE BERLIN GAOL: INMATES AND MURDER MOST DEADLY

She had not known the weight until she felt the freedom.

— Nathaniel Hawthorne

BY THE EARLY 1850s, Berlin was a thriving community whose urban development depended as much upon the influx of new immigrants as it did on the economic stability of those who had founded it.

Times were changing and, along with them, the infrastructure. Out of the bush had emerged a vibrant urban core — the earliest corduroy roads had, for the most part, given way to modernized streets and alleys. Merchants offered goods that previously were attainable only from outside the region. Hotels, offering a staggering array of foods and services, serviced both visitors and locals looking for a good meal. Factories were booming and employment opportunities were plenty. Schools and churches were well attended, financed by the economic generosity of a successful merchant class.

With the increase in prosperity and as the population grew, there was a burgeoning desire among local citizens to administer their own legal affairs.

Many were tired of travelling out of town to conduct official business. It was time, the local citizenry said, to have a courthouse of their own, and Berliners decided to apply to the provincial government for their own county seat. Friedrich Gaukel, a strong community investor and one of the area's foremost landowners, supported the successful petition in 1852 (the same year as the inception of Waterloo County) by donating two and a half acres for the construction of the new county buildings — first a courthouse and then the Waterloo County Gaol. The city still owns this original land parcel, which borders on Queen, Frederick, and Weber Streets in downtown Kitchener.

As with the courthouse, the "Gaol" — or jail — did convey a certain status and independence for the community, but the community's desire for such an institution was not simply linked to civic pride. The quickly developing Waterloo subscribed to the belief that it was necessary to have publicly funded institutions to incarcerate or otherwise control those deemed criminal, dangerous, or unfit, in order to better guarantee "public safety." Of course, once a jail is built, it's likely that more and more reasons will be found to actually use it.

By 1852 the community had various transient homeless "tramps," as they were called. Not all of them were adults: most were men, some were women and some were orphaned children. Some suffered from age-related debilities, others from some form of physical or mental disability, some from alcohol addiction. In general, all suffered from a lack of medical care, as well as access to facilities to maintain hygiene.

Marginalized by poverty, the homeless would work at menial jobs when they could find them; when they couldn't, they would be forced to struggle — begging on the streets, sometimes entering shops to beg from the customers and the proprietor. It was not at all unusual for homeless women to resort to prostitution. Orphaned children sometimes joined together and got involved in a number of petty crimes — theft, pickpocketing, and property damage.

Many of the tramps were dirty, smelly, and sometimes lousy, and were thus objects of disgust. All were socially alienated. They were seen as a "problem" and a nuisance. With no other real social welfare provisions in place at that time, a jail was seen as providing a means of getting some of these folks off the street — at least temporarily.

It should be noted that, at one time, rural Mennonites had their own solution to transients. Many Mennonite farm homes had a reserved space in their homes where they would provide a bed for the night and food in exchange for chores around the farm. For them, this was a practical way to practise their faith — offering charity and a "hand up" to those in need. Both the Joseph Schneider Haus Museum and the Peter Martin House at the Doon Heritage Village in Kitchener include an interpretive narrative about how tramps were treated by the Mennonites when they came knocking at the doors in the early years of Waterloo County. In some cases the tramps were seasonal visitors who returned annually. They became acquainted with particular rural Mennonite families, who anticipated their return. Some of these tramps engaged in the decorative folk-art practice known as "chip carving" (most commonly using old wooden cigar boxes), leaving behind lovely examples of their work as gifts for their hosts in appreciation for their kindness. Examples of these boxes have often been featured in exhibits and collections throughout the region, and in some cases, stories of their creators have been included.

The practice in town was decidedly different, though. In July 1852 council approved the proposal that a jail be built, and a contract was awarded to the Brantford architectural firm Mellish & Russel. The building, which cost £4,875.00, was designed in the Greek Classical Revival style. The two-storey stone building presented an interesting dilemma almost immediately upon opening — overcrowding. Opening in January of 1853, the jail instantly filled up. Thirty-eight men and one woman were crammed into a limited holding space that featured fourteen single cells and six double ones. Not only was the size of the jail inadequate from the beginning, there was also no wall outside the perimeter of the exercise yard.

Upgrades were undertaken, construction oversights corrected, and necessary amenities installed over time. A few months after the jail opened, a tender for £197 and 55 shillings was received by Abram Tyson (a local merchant) to construct and install iron gratings for ten windows, and to build both a wooden perimeter fence and a cistern for rainwater collection. A fourteen-foot-high stone wall was constructed around the exercise yard in 1861.

In the early years the jail had no indoor kitchen (some cooking was done outside in a makeshift kitchen), and many prisoners relied on food brought to them by family members and loved ones. A 1984 archaeological dig revealed, among other things, various domestic remnants of the more civilized life that existed beyond the prisoners' jail cell walls: china plates, tea cups, saucers, and glass bottles. An array of clay pipes were also uncovered that would have belonged to both male and female inmates. A kitchen and store room were built in 1861 and, in 1863, a washing machine was purchased at a cost of about £7.5.

In 1878 a residence was constructed on the property to house the chief administrative officer, Jonathan Cook, also known as the "Gaoler" or "Governor" of the jail. This "Governor's House" was an impressive mid-Victorian Italianate-style mansion reflective of the governor's prominent position within the community. The home was an extravagant indulgence, but the citizens of Berlin were eager to demonstrate their growing prosperity. The mansion's interior featured beautifully carved woodwork, and spiral staircases that led to the upper floors. The main-floor fireplace was enhanced by a marble mantelpiece.

Although a kitchen was eventually installed in the jail, the prisoners' diet was only barely improved. Even in the early 1900s, for example, prison rations consisted of just two meals a day. The breakfast meal was simply a pint of oatmeal gruel and eight ounces of bread. Dinner was a bit more substantial and would have featured a pint of soup and eight ounces of bread. Two days a week, inmates would receive an additional five ounces of cooked meat and one and a half pounds of potatoes. Animal bones retrieved during the archaeological dig showed that cheap cuts of meat were used to make stew: mutton, pork, and white-tailed deer, which was once ubiquitous throughout the region and pretty much free for the taking.

Although most of the prisoners were males, there were some females admitted for incarceration — not always because they had been found guilty of a crime. Israel Bowman, the county clerk, recorded an incident in his day book of a sixteen-year-old girl whose father had approached the magistrate and requested she be locked up in case she "entered into a life of ill-repute." The reason? She had refused to marry an older man of her father's choosing.

As with most jails, escapes were common enough and, by today's standards, almost comical. One prisoner, whose name was Haywood, escaped by piling buckets one on top of another on a bench, then climbing up them and jumping over the stone wall of the exercise yard. As the story goes, he left the premises simply by going through the front gate, because the turnkey had left it unlocked when he went to Sunday School.

Those inmates who did not escape were often subjected to back-breaking work. Some were sent out to work in factories that benefited from the "cheap" labour. By 1899 prisoners were slugging it out by breaking rocks for local contractors — both as a way for the jail to help defray its costs and also as a deterrent for beggars. Local tramps and wandering homeless people (who had not broken any law except perhaps the almost-never-enforced law against loitering) would show up at the jail, particularly in the cold months, looking for free lodging and a meal. Not all of them qualified for admission to the Waterloo County House of Industry and Refuge (as I will discuss in the next chapter), which would have been the logical choice to house the poor and needy, and some of the voluntary jail applicants didn't want to go there, anyway. Begging still allowed for some autonomy, albeit very little, since relying on charity from others, of any kind, was a risk — there was no guarantee beggars would receive anything and there was a chance they could get beaten up or killed in the process of being a "nuisance." Jail administrators hoped that beggars would see the hard labour of the prisoners, be put off by the prospect, and move to "other counties." ("Not in my back yard....") It was reported to council that this strategy had been successful in reducing the number of tramps throughout the county.

Of course, it was not only tramps and beggars who were locked up in the Waterloo County Gaol. In fact, there were many ways one could end up in jail, especially since it was the first (and only) source of social welfare in Waterloo County. Some were committed because of physical infirmity and some for mental infirmity (this was before the construction of "insane" asylums). Jailing those with mental disabilities and those suffering from psychological disorders, particularly those who were more violent or physically threatening, served to get some of them off the streets. It helped to provide peace of mind to the general public, who may have found such people disturbing (or downright threatening), but it did nothing to help those who were suffering, particularly if they had a secondary problem like alcohol addiction, which destroyed not only the bodies and minds of the alcoholics but also their social relationships, potential support systems (family members who may have had enough), and most certainly their self-esteem.

Alcohol was widely available and generally cheap to buy. In the nineteenth century temperance reformers loudly decried the evils of alcohol as the root cause of any number of social problems such as crime, unemployment, violence, poverty, public intoxication, and insanity. Locally, Joseph E. Schneider, a temperance sympathizer, would rent out land for temperance meetings near what is today Charles and Queen Streets during the 1840s and 1850s.

Many of the inmates in the County Gaol had been admitted in an intoxicated state. More often than not, they were also charged with instigating or being involved in violence against others, general larceny, and burglary while intoxicated.

A more unfortunate reason for incarceration was debt. Insolvent people who could not pay their debts were sometimes subjected to jail time, their possessions confiscated and summarily sold off to pay their creditors. Some of these debtors desperately tried to hold on to their assets and property, but the financial system of the day was a harsh one. As a result, it sometimes led to acts of desperation — as evidenced by the tragic end of Frank Schmitt.

Frank Schmitt had fallen on hard times. The owner of Schmitt's Lager Beer Saloon was a desperate man. In the frigid temperatures on January 17, 1862, fire engines were dispatched at around 1:30 a.m. as reports of a blaze indicated that the saloon on Walter Street North in Galt was engulfed in flames. At the coroner's inquest, held the day after the fire, it was revealed that Frank was more than a few months behind on his property payments and that he had been seen removing a number of belongings from the premises in the days preceding the blaze. Further, witnesses testified that Frank had been seen walking quickly down the street away from the saloon around the time the fire was reported. Frank and his wife were both arrested and sent to jail to await trial on charges of incendiarism. Frank was a broken man and never made it to trial. He died by suicide on February 5, 1862, in his cell, leaving his wife to face the charges alone.

Frank's story is only one of many. Acts of arson have continued to plague Waterloo's downtown core into even more recent years, sometimes connected to insurance fraud.

* * *

The most serious crime for which people were incarcerated was, of course, murder. Committing murder was one of the few crimes punishable by death. In the later 1800s the sentence for first-degree murder was death by hanging. (The death penalty was removed from the Criminal Code in 1976.)

It is bitterly ironic that the reason the Waterloo County Gaol has been preserved is that those convicted of murder in the adjacent court used to be executed and buried in the jail's yard.

Three hangings took place at the Waterloo County Gaol, roughly twenty years apart — in 1898, 1920, and 1940. All the bodies were buried in the exercise yard near where the gallows had been. This was a common practice in early jails. If the executed prisoner's body wasn't claimed upon death by a friend or family member, then the body was interred in the jail yard. So, the jail yard became a de facto cemetery.

The first person executed was a seventeen-year-old boy known as "Simpering Jim" James Allison. It was said that his lips formed a "simpering" expression, "like that of a cat.") He was also called "the chore boy," because at the time of the murder he was the hired hand of Anthony Orr.

This is a rather sad story, not only because Jim was still a teen at the time of the murder (and his execution) but because there was ample evidence that Jim was developmentally challenged, or "dull-witted," and so may not have fully understood the gravity of the crime he was convicted of committing.

The victim was Mrs. Anthony Orr (née Emma Borland), the wife of his employer. One theory regarding the motive for the murder was that Jim made a pass at Emma and she rejected him, causing him to fly into a rage and kill her in a moment of passion. When Jim confessed to the killing, he claimed he did it while he was doing his chores and denied having come on to her. Another account says that Emma's husband, Tony Orr, had refused to let Jim go with the Orr family on a trip to Niagara Falls and that Jim became angry and vengeful because of it.

There are a few details of the case that are indisputable. Emma was described as being "a beauty," who was friendly and outgoing. She came from a well-to-do family and had been previously married. There was common knowledge about Emma's past (and present) involvement with other men. Tony knew that his wife loved excitement and travel — so much that she had once left him to run off with one of their hired hands named Mullholland. Tony had gone looking for her and had found Emma and their two children in Niagara Falls. Described as a nervous, excitable man, Tony had had trouble with other men because of his wife's straying. There was gossip that many men came and went at the Orr farmhouse when Tony wasn't home. On the occasion of the Mullolland affair, Tony convinced Emma to come home with him and reconcile.

One August morning two years later, Tony left with his nine-year-old son, Norman, to sell a sow. His wife, ten-year-old daughter, Maggie, and their one-year-old baby were left behind at home. Tony said he'd be back in a couple of hours. Two hours later Tony returned to his house, but instead of Emma, he ran into a laughing Jim Allison. Not making much sense, Jim claimed Tony's wife was "gone" but didn't elaborate much when Tony questioned him repeatedly. He just kept laughing. Tony launched a search for Emma, even going to the home of one of her suitors — who was alone and claimed he hadn't seen her that day. Tony returned home and called the authorities. There were rumours of her having committed suicide.

A week went by without a word of Emma's whereabouts. The police continued their search. Three men, including Allison, were under surveillance and were considered to be suspects in her disappearance. Tony was quickly ruled out as he had been five miles away in the company of his son and another farmer while he sold the sow. He was nowhere near the farm when Emma disappeared. The other two suspects also turned out to have been somewhere else at the time, leaving Allison as suspect number one.

During a search of the Orr farm property, a detective noticed that one of the perimeter fence pickets had been broken off. Beyond the broken fencing was a swamp. Between the house and the swamp was a corn patch. One of the rows was raised in one section. Disturbing the soil with his foot, Tony's brother, John, uncovered Emma six inches below the surface, buried face down. The grave had been a makeshift, temporary one, quickly dug. The police believed that the murderer had intended to come back and hide Emma later, in the swamp.

A further turn of events added to the incriminating evidence that was mounting against Jim. The police had his bloodstained shotgun, and Tony's brother John had said that he had heard a shot just after Tony had left.

Emma had been shot, then clubbed to death. It was established that her murder had been clumsy, quick, and that her killer had done it in a fit of rage. Jim Allison was arrested. During the trial, it was revealed that Jim's father, Alex, had followed his son to the swamp the night of the murder, intending to finish digging a proper grave. Beside this new grave, Jim had left behind a footprint and his knife.

Apparently Jim learned to read and write in the jail during the six months while he awaited his fate. He wrote a letter of admission and apology for his actions, which he read aloud before he ascended the scaffold. He died by hanging on February 4, 1898. He was eighteen when he was executed.

The next man executed for murder was Stoyko Boyeff, who went to the gallows in 1920. A recent immigrant from Bulgaria, he was described as being very hot-tempered. Apparently, Boyeff had had an argument with a Russian immigrant, John Soroksty, in a quarry. Soroksty's body was found there some time later and the cause of his death was attributed to stoning. Since Boyeff was the last known person to be seen with Soroksty alive (and someone who had been seen arguing with him where the murder took place), Boyeff was arrested. Although he made no public confession, he bragged in jail to some visiting friends about killing Soroksty. Later, at his trial, their testimony was used against him. He was convicted of the murder and sentenced to hang. There was some discussion about Boyeff's command of the English language, especially since his conviction relied heavily on his friends' testimony, not his own. Regardless, Boyeff, like Jim Allison, died at the end of a rope and was also buried in the exercise yard of the jail.

The final execution that took place at the jail was that of convicted axe murder Reginald White. A former resident of Hespeler, White was accused of murdering an elderly farmer for whom he had worked, John Milroy, as well as his blind sister, Annie Milroy. Upon his arrest, White indicated that he had been recently engaged to a local girl and that, desperate for money, he had gone to John Milroy seeking $500 in back pay for jobs he had done several years previously but for which he had not received compensation. A scuffle ensued between the younger White and elderly John Milroy.

White had taken a gun to the Milroys — perhaps because he felt that he might need to threaten the farmer in order to induce him to pay the debt — but it had been loaded with the wrong bullets and was useless. He grabbed the closest thing — an axe — and started swinging. Annie had been sleeping and it was believed that the noise woke her up. When she came downstairs, she, too, met Reg and the axe.

The police said that the killing was clumsy and spontaneous. A psychiatrist testified at the trial that White's intelligence was low but he knew right from wrong. The judge, upon receiving the determination of the jury, shed a tear as he sentenced young White to the gallows, saying, "You have been found guilty of a most cowardly crime." On April 25, 1940, Reginald White climbed the scaffold for the first and last time. He, too, was not claimed upon death and is believed to have been buried in the jail yard.

The Waterloo County Gaol was in continuous use and operation from when it opened in 1853 until 1978, when it was shut down because of its outdated and somewhat dilapidated condition. The Governor's House also remained empty. Both were forgotten for a few years, neglected, and slated for the wrecking ball. A dedicated group of built-heritage supporters, though, determined to save both buildings, formed a Friends of the Governor's House and Waterloo County Gaol. The owner of both buildings was the Region of Waterloo, and it wanted to tear the buildings down to make room for a parking lot. From a historical and architectural point of view, this would have been a significant loss. The 1852 jail was the oldest civic building in the city. The architectural features of the Governor's House were distinct and also worthy of preservation. But, how to save them?

The committee, chaired by Jean Haalboom, a former regional councillor, valiantly engaged community support for the buildings. They argued that before demolition could occur the city had to search the property for the bodies of the three men interred there. The region agreed to order an archaeological survey of the property in order to look for the bodies. This was conducted in 1986.

The former Waterloo County Gaol in 1985.

Along with the many artifacts, the bodies of two of the three deceased criminals, Jim Allison and Stoyko Boyeff, were found. Witnesses still living and who had seen the actual execution, gave a description of Boyeff's burial that assisted the team in eventually finding the bodies. The two bodies were disinterred and reburied in Woodland Cemetery in Kitchener.

Reginald White's body has remained elusive. It is believed that White's body was buried under 136 kilograms of lump lime, which may have contributed to its decomposition. The Governor's House and the Gaol escaped demolition, but White's body became the subject of an extensive search of the former exercise yard. Numerous areas were excavated.

Today, the jail has been renovated for use as a municipal courtroom and office space. The Governor's House has also been restored and is now the home of the Waterloo Region Crime Prevention Council. Artifacts from the dig are on display in a glass case in the entrance. The former exercise yard has been beautifully landscaped and provides a seating place surrounded by a well-cultivated garden.

But the exact whereabouts of Reg White's body still remain a mystery.

6

THE WATERLOO COUNTY HOUSE OF INDUSTRY AND REFUGE: CASE STUDIES IN CONTRAST

> The most terrible poverty is loneliness and the feeling of being unloved.
>
> — Mother Theresa

THE 1867 *ONTARIO MUNICIPAL ACT* required all municipalities to provide support for residents in need of assistance. Those who qualified for assistance — in the parlance of the day, those deemed "burdens on society" — included the poor, the aged and infirm, and minor children who were either orphaned, abandoned, or members of a family who couldn't (or wouldn't) support them. This lack of support was the result of many things, such as poverty, disability (of the child or the caregiver), death of the caregiver, and family breakdown.

Family breakdown itself had several causes. Desertion was a problem; divorce was sometimes an issue, too. Mental illness, domestic violence, and criminal activity also contributed. Extreme poverty exerted overwhelming pressure on an already disadvantaged population; it also resulted in the breakdown of many marriages.

Whatever the cause for their predicament, by the late nineteenth century those in need of assistance were turning more and more to government for support. For the residents of Waterloo County, getting these people off the streets was a priority. In anticipation of financial assistance from the government in fulfillment of Section 413 of the *Ontario Municipal Act*, the County of Waterloo Council began to look for a suitable location to build a House of Industry and Refuge, or HIR.

In October of 1867, council purchased 141 acres from John Eby for $9,024. John Eby's farm was about a kilometre from the Waterloo County Court House and Gaol, so the location was ideal. Ninety-seven acres of the property had been cleared and forty-four remained untouched woodland. There was also a house on the property.

Council advertised for a contractor and, in 1868 hired Louis Kribs to build the facility. The contract cost almost as much as the land purchase: $8,098.00. All of the labour to build the main building was supplied by local workers (many of whom were related in some way to the members of the county council). The House opened on June 15, 1869, and the first residents admitted were primarily homeless children and unwed mothers. The original building had the capacity to house one hundred inmates.

Originally designed as a self-sufficient facility — it had an on-site farm — HIR never lived up to that expectation. In the end, the growing town of Berlin's need for vacant land trumped HIR's requirement for its farm land, and much of the institution's property was sold off. The idea of a self-sufficient facility did not die easily, however. Trying to maintain the dream, HIR acquired three adjacent farms, including the Shuh and Weber farms. The Frederick Street location cared for those who were chronically ill, while those who were destitute but still able-bodied worked and lived on the farms, raising livestock and various crops. Residents were required to work for their keep. Expenses were costed out at $1.34 per person per week. Responsibility for the financial affairs of the House changed over time, but was it was mostly the shared responsibility of the County of Waterloo and its townships. A keeper/manager and a matron lived at the House and managed its daily operations as well as the working farms.

Between its opening in 1869 and its closure in 1957, it is estimated that approximately 3,200 people lived at HIR. The length of stay for residents varied — some stayed for a little as a day and others resided there for most of their lives. For example, the first person admitted to the HIR was a sick fifty-five-year-old labourer named James White. He died just thirty-one days later. In another example, as we have seen, the ex-slave Levi Carroll's stepdaughter, Emiline, entered the House along with Levi and her son, William Aylestock, in 1891. Levi died there in 1897. William left when he reached his teens and went on to marry and have children of his own. Emiline, deemed infirm, lived at the House until her death in 1945. Their stories were not unique: some residents were born in the HIR and others clearly died there. Some of those who died were very young and ill children who had entered the House in a desperate, near-death state. One was an eleven-day-old infant who weighed just three pounds (even with his clothes on). "Charlie" had been left on someone's doorstep before he was surrendered to the House. For these, nothing much could be done, except perhaps to provide burial.

For those who died at the HIR, there were two cemeteries over the years. The first, in use from 1869 until 1884, was located north of the railroad tracks that ran parallel to Wilmot Street (today, Victoria Street). In 1884 another cemetery was opened up; this was bordered by Dunham Avenue and Victoria, Mansion, and Indiana Streets. This cemetery was in use until 1907. These cemeteries present an abiding mystery for those seeking to find who was buried there. For one thing, there are no markers. A glance through the HIR burial register indicates that numbers were assigned for graves, but, without markers, finding the exact location is nearly impossible.

There is another, and perhaps more disturbing, anomaly. The graves were supposed to have been moved when the cemeteries ceased operation. The problem is that no extant records indicate that this was ever done — in fact, the evidence suggests that at least some (and maybe most) of the bodies buried in the cemeteries were never moved.

That's right.

In 1941, while excavating a new cellar on Dunham Avenue, a worker unearthed two skeletons, interred in rough coffins, which were later identified as an adult male and a child who had died sometime in the late 1860s. Following the Second World War, as a number of new houses were being constructed along Dunham Street, more bodies were unearthed. There is speculation that there are also some that remain undetected. As recently as 1966, an excavation at the former Electrohome site on Wellington Street uncovered a body (reportedly from the first HIR cemetery, north of the tracks). During the 1960s, a skull was unearthed at a property on Dunham.

By 1913 the potter's fields were no longer being used, and unclaimed bodies were sent to the Toronto School of Anatomy, where medical students would use them for dissection. Diary accounts from residents of the House reveal that some of them were terrified that, without their consent, this is what would happen to them when they died. It was a distinct possibility, since the prevailing social attitude of the day was that the indigent and others needing assistance were of little value and therefore had no right to control what happened to them — or to their bodies after death. It is almost certain that the practice of sending of bodies to the Toronto School of Anatomy began quite early, as legislation allowed for unclaimed bodies of people who died in provincially funded facilities to be forwarded to a medical school for the furthering of anatomical science (via dissection).

Over the years, the main building was expanded and renovated to accommodate more inmates, as well as modern utilities like furnaces and electrical wiring. In time, an isolation hospital, referred to as the "pest house" was added to the property, as were a chapel and more storage barns. The isolation hospital accommodated those who needed to be kept apart from the general population because of the possibility that they would spread contagions like tuberculosis, smallpox, or diphtheria.

Though this house was built to accommodate the needs of Waterloo County residents, other municipalities were notorious for offloading their own indigent populations to any area that had a poorhouse — Wellington and Waterloo Counties, Toronto, etc. At one point, the local county council decided that at least in one instance they were going to crack down on the practice: they refused to take incoming transfers from Stratford. (Stratford eventually built its own House of Industry, about 1904.)

* * *

Gaining entrance into the HIR was not a matter of simply turning up at the institution's door. In order to be accepted (or committed), one of the following had to approve the application and the individual for entrance: the reeve, the deputy reeve, the warden or inspector of the HIR, or either of two justices of the peace commissioned within Waterloo County. If none of these approved the application, then the applicant could be refused entry. This would have placed a desperate person in an untenable situation, particularly in the winter.

Applicants had to list the reason for applying, known as the "cause of pauperism." The reasons listed varied widely and included such things as sickness, destitution, intemperance, lameness, old age, blindness, "parents gaoled," vagrancy, being orphaned, and being "idiotic or an imbecile."

Some inmates of the HIR had served time in the Waterloo County Gaol prior to entering the House. Others, deemed insane, were sometimes admitted for a short stay in the HIR before being shipped off to a facility that provided for the care of the "mentally ill, criminally insane, and the feeble-minded." Transferring these folks wasn't cheap, and sometimes the bill was forwarded to their families to pay.

Those admitted as inmates were separated by sex upon entrance. Women and children were housed separately from men. This segregation did nothing to strengthen family ties or personal well-being. Children were sometimes sent out to work at placements, to earn money for their upkeep, and others were adopted out (sometimes without prior parental approval). Women who could do so worked in the House providing the domestic duties that included mending, ironing, cleaning, and laundry. Men worked when and if they could at menial tasks. One disabled elderly man, William Smith, who walked on his knees, split all the wood used in the HIR and also made wooden clothes pegs and toys for the children.

Though the conditions experienced by the general population of the institutions were bad, those faced by the black population and the mentally ill were significantly worse. They suffered from discrimination and extra abuse. Of course, this situation was simply the product of the general prejudice that existed in society as a whole.

This attitude is exemplified in the writings of William Jaffray. Born in England, Jaffray immigrated to Galt sometime between 1840 and 1850, along with his parents and five of his siblings (a sixth was born in Galt a few years later). William worked for the *Berlin Chronicle* and *Galt Reporter* in the 1860s, at first as a bookkeeper and then as both a journalist and an editor. He was particularly community-minded, becoming postmaster and later mayor of Berlin. Indeed, at times he held multiple political positions.

Jaffray developed an interest in the HIR shortly after it opened, when he was the deputy reeve of Berlin. One of his duties was to commit people to the House. Sometimes, he was required to send paupers elsewhere and approve payment for their travel expenses. The daily operation of the House, and its inmates, greatly piqued his interest, and in 1871 he decided to spend a full day there in order to appreciate more fully how things worked. He later wrote an article about it and presented his findings in a town hall speech a month later.

Jaffray offered praise for the overall administration and operation of the House. He noted the "care" the institution provided for its inmates, referring to the food they ate and the large rooms they lived in; he also endorsed the imposition and enforcement of specific rules, which he said provided and reinforced stability and order. Disturbingly, he confirmed that inmates were locked in their rooms at night (as if it were a jail).

In his article he comments repeatedly, in a condescending way, on various manners and behaviours of the people housed in the HIR. He describes how the people lined up for their food — after a long night, I am sure that they were hungry. He wonders at their passive complacency at receiving and eating their food during breakfast time. He continues his observations, pausing at intervals to criticize and comment on some inmates' various physical and mental health issues. He refers to the day room as the "day room for idiots," and states that the shaving of the residents was "a waste on the pauper crowds," as if hygiene were neither required nor desired by (or for) the inmates.

What is perhaps most offensive about Jaffray's article is the racism evident when he mentions two black residents of the HIR: Albert Hunt and William Robinson. He never met Hunt, but because Hunt had impressed staff with his pleasant ways and hard work ethic, Jaffrey was somewhat more "kind" to him in his observations. He lamented the fact that Hunt had been recently released from the HIR, which resulted in Jaffray not being able to meet with him personally: "I was disappointed, for the old darkey's relatives had relieved him from the Poor House a short time before. I am told that Albert Hunt was one of the most useful and genial inmates of the House...."

In contrast, Jaffray's tone was sharp when he wrote of William Robinson: "This darkey was good for nothing — a perfect black drone in the hive ... whiskey told him to come down and the coon dropped without waiting for another discharge of fire water...."

The negative attitude in Jaffray's writing may have been common, but it was not universal. There is evidence that kindness and respect was offered to black citizens in Waterloo County — at least at times and by some. For example, the treatment offered to the ex-slave Levi Carroll (whose story was covered in detail earlier) seems to have been much better than it was for many of his contemporaries. Levi was elderly, in his nineties, and disabled when he entered the HIR. He lived there for six years until he died, but the two obituaries published on different days by different people spoke very favourably about him. It is true that his treatment in the House may not have been positive, but it is safe to say that in death he was respected and honourably remembered.

The mistreatment and discrimination suffered by the mentally challenged was particularly awful. In this, Jaffray was not the only one to offer abuse. The experience of the Groff family is a perfect example of how those with mental disabilities were mistreated by the institutions that were supposed to aid them.

The Groff family had several children with mental disabilities, all of whom were committed together. Initially, they were housed in the House of Industry. There were eleven children in the family. Four of the eleven were listed as "being of unsound mind." The staff at the HIR referred to the four as the "Groff Idiots." On their entrance application, the cause of their pauperism was inscribed as "idiotic." The children had been there for about nine months when the inspector of the House tried to extract money from their family and friends for their care and maintenance. No one paid. Eventually, the children were sent to the Hamilton Insane Asylum; but soon after, they were returned to the HIR. This stay was a short one also, as they were sent back to Hamilton only a month later. It was clear that local staff wanted nothing to do with them. Finally, Hamilton relocated the children to the Asylum for Idiots and Feeble-Minded in Orillia, where they lived for the rest of their lives. Other Groff family members came and went at the HIR, including the father, but most stayed only a short period of time.

There were also inmates who came from prominent families. It is not fully known how or why all of them came to be there. For example, several

Jacob Gaukel Stroh photograph of August Drexler (Drechsler) c. 1900.

members of the Hibner family lived and died in the House. Daniel Hibner was a mayor of Berlin during the late 1890s and served in numerous political positions, sometimes committing people to the HIR. One of his relations, Susannah Hibner, was admitted to the HIR and was listed as being of "weak intellect, an imbecile." Susannah died only one month after her committal, from cancer, at age twenty-seven. Was the cancer the reason for her mental challenges? We will likely never know.

One eccentric inmate, August Drexler, was an accomplished violinist who seems to have fallen on hard times. He was apparently a bit of a wanderer, as one of his friends claimed he told him, following an evening concert, that he was taking his leave to walk the more than seventeen miles to Wellesley. Another time, he claimed to have gotten off the train in Walkerton and walked for two days back to Berlin.

Drexler must have had some financial means, as he would stay in hotels as well as with friends whenever he was not staying at the House of Industry. There is some possibility that he had at least mild dementia — he would write undecipherable markings for hours and claim to be writing music. He was a free spirit and a stubborn one, who sometimes let his hair, clothing, and hygiene go. When asked by the renowned Professor Theo Zoellner to play in his orchestra, Drexler was informed that clean and appropriate attire would be expected, and a bath. He consented and arrived as a clean-cut, distinguished-looking gentleman. When not playing, however, he let his hair grow and wandered around barefoot or in slippers (and sometimes in rather scanty clothing).

In 1919 the House of Industry began to transition away from its provisional care of the poor, moving steadily toward the care of the elderly. In 1947 the Ontario *Homes for the Aged Act* mandated that institutions provide care for the elderly. The House of Industry became known as the Waterloo County Home for the Aged.

In time, other social welfare programs offered supports to those in need, making the HIR obsolete. In 1962 the Salvation Army purchased the building to construct the A.R. Goudie Eventide Home. As for the Waterloo

Waterloo County House of Industry and Refuge c. 1900.

County Home for the Aged, it moved to Franklin Street in Kitchener. Today it is known as the Sunnyside Foundation, and is owned and operated by the Region of Waterloo. It offers a variety of programs: some live-in residential options supply supportive housing, while other initiatives are oriented toward support for dementia and other long-term care needs that are age-related.

7

CONTAINMENT FOR CHILDREN: THE ORPHANAGES

> The little people must be sacred to the big ones, and it is from the rights of the weak that the duty of the strong is comprised.
>
> — Victor Hugo

BY THE 1920s AND '30s there were at least three orphanages operating in Waterloo County. One was faith-based (Roman Catholic), one was publicly owned, and the other was privately owned (although donations and support came from various organizations and church groups). They were the St. Agatha Orphanage, the Kitchener-Waterloo Orphanage, and the Coombe Orphanage in Hespeler (formerly a receiving home for children who came to Canada from Smyly Homes in Ireland).*

* In a 1896 provincial report on Children's Protection and Home-Finding, there is mention of another facility — the Wellesley Orphanage — operated by the German Lutherans, which housed fifteen children on that date. However, I will be focusing in this chapter on the three facilities mentioned above.

CHILDREN'S SOCIAL WELFARE PROGRAMS AND INSTITUTIONS

Until the mid- to late nineteenth century, Ontarians depended largely upon various charitable organizations, volunteers, and local community groups to provide support and care for abandoned, orphaned, or neglected children. Some children were runaways from abusive home situations, while others had been abandoned or orphaned upon the death of their parents, or had no close relative to take them in in their time of need.

By the latter half of the nineteenth century, the situation had changed somewhat, and some of the children were placed in orphanages or shelters that were often staffed by volunteers. Some orphaned children were "lucky" and were got apprenticeships that included room and board in return for their domestic service or manual labour. Unfortunately, all too often, they were taken advantage of as cheap labour, and were routinely ill-treated.

The degree to which the children were exploited as cheap labour is made clear when one examines their wages. Recommended wages for girls in domestic service in the 1890s ranged from about two to six dollars per month. For boys, as apprentices or labourers, wages were slightly higher: three to six dollars per month. In contrast, adult male farm labourers then would make about twenty dollars per month and adult female domestic workers about eleven dollars. Their situations were largely the same as those for the children, since both would include some kind of room and board in addition to the earned wage.

Any exploitation was almost universally unnoted by the many "godly citizens" who helped to provide funding for the orphanages. They did not see (or chose not to see) the abuses heaped upon children — the respectable citizens were content if they could be seen to be providing charitable donations and, perhaps, campaigning against injustice. For the most part, these patrons of the poor preferred to keep their distance from those they claimed to be interested in helping; they did not wish to actually visit the placements or children in them.

In 1895 the amended *Act for the Prevention of Cruelty to, and Better Protection of, Children* laid out that every town that had a population of ten thousand people or more must provide for a shelter or receiving home to offer temporary care for children apprehended by authorities (and in holding) until suitable shelter could be found. By 1930 more than eight hundred children were living some kind of temporary shelter in Ontario. By the end of the Second World War, shelters were being phased out in favour of a group-home model of care that proposed a shift toward fewer residents per adult caregiver, that was supposed to mimic a home, rather than an industrial, impersonal institution. (Foster care had already emerged by the latter half of the nineteenth century, even though foster children were still often used as domestics or labourers within their foster homes).

Orphaned or abandoned children were contained in charitably funded orphanages, and there were also prison-schools or reformatories, established in the mid-nineteenth century, for children who displayed criminal tendencies. The reformatories were to house those children who had been labelled as criminals, and correct this behaviour through discipline. A later shift in reform philosophy that moved from punishment to rescue led to the formation of industrial schools. Children fourteen years old and under, otherwise homeless and guilty of a petty crime, could be sent to the

St. Agatha Orphanage

industrial school, where they were housed and schooled in academics and life skills. Since many of these children had experienced great neglect (and traumatic abuse), many were lacking in even the most elementary social skills. Industrial-school training was intended to provide stability and care in a more residential, cottage-type setting than the harsher reformatories.

There were also the orphanages that were intended to provide care for children in need until they could be adopted out to permanent homes.

Locally, three orphanages stand out.

ST. AGATHA ORPHANAGE AND FATHER EUGENE FUNCKEN

In 1834 Father John Wiriath established a Roman Catholic mission in St. Agatha. The mission was originally housed in a two-room log building that initially, served as both a school and a church. In time, a larger frame church was constructed to replace the log building. This was expanded and modified over the years as different priests served and left their marks on the community. By 1848 a brick rectory was established, followed by a two-storey stone school in 1854 (that also provided living space for teachers).

Perhaps the man with the most enduring effect upon the mission up until that point was Father Eugene Funcken. Funcken is credited with numerous initiatives, including the erection of a cemetery chapel and shrine (to welcome observant pilgrims), the building of St. Jerome's College (1864), and the establishment of an institution that is locally recognized to this day — the St. Agatha Orphanage.

Funcken founded the orphanage in 1858 along with assistance of women in the local community. There had been a devastating fire in St. Agatha village that year, and nine (some accounts say ten) children were left without homes or their parents. Funcken stepped in to help. By 1868 a stone chapel and dormitory was added to the property on donated land next to the church. A functioning building had been created to house the orphans, but Funcken needed help to run the orphanage, and so, two years later, he travelled to Wisconsin to request the help of the School Sisters of Notre Dame to see if they would come and administer the orphanage and school by providing guidance and teaching to the children. They agreed.

Another school building was built in 1875, and by 1902, a brick residence. The citizens of St. Agatha provided much of the financial support for the orphanage for many years. Locals also held working bees to provide for the needs of the children. One such event was an annual "butchering bee," in which volunteers prepared enough meat to supply the orphanage for the entire winter. Sometimes the meat was donated from local farms. After preparation, the meat could be frozen for winter use.

The orphanage as such closed in 1965, when the facility became a residential treatment centre for "emotionally disturbed" children. Cottages provided the housing for children and "live-in" counsellors. Locally known as "the Children's Village," the orphanage continued to be run by nuns; however, they ceased administrative responsibility for the facility in 1968. Today, counselling for the children and their families continues to be offered, though now it is provided through a variety of services, many of which partner with community agencies like Lutherwood. Today, the facility operates as a non-profit named KidsLINK.

THE BERLIN ORPHANAGE (ALSO KNOWN AS THE KITCHENER-WATERLOO ORPHANAGE AND, LATER, WILLOW HALL)

On May 30, 1896, there was a meeting at the Berlin YMCA. Those in attendance recognized that the time had come to provide for the needs of orphaned children in the community. Fifteen hundred dollars was summarily raised for the opening of what would become the Berlin Orphanage. (The orphanage had really begun a few months previous when Mrs. A. Stoltz, wife of a United Brethren Church minister, took some children into the couple's home on Frederick Street in Kitchener. The reverend Stoltz and his wife were soon in over their heads and realized that they needed help.)

The group used the funding raised to buy its first building at King and Wilmot (today, Victoria) Streets and there the facility opened in December 1896. It operated at this location until it moved in 1923 to larger accommodation on Charles Street — by then, in Kitchener.

The first matron was an unlikely candidate but ended up being a godsend. Nearly thirty-four years old and unmarried, Miss Mary Snider was the daughter of a farmer, born just outside Waterloo. Appointed as the first matron of the Berlin Orphanage, Mary was given the salary of eight dollars a month. This was lower than even the domestic wages, previously mentioned, for adult females working in a domestic field at this time. Despite the low pay, the position was still a desirable one. Mary, as the key administrator for the institution, had considerable independence and social responsibility — things that many women of her age or class would not have had. Mary had two assistants whose salary was six dollars each per month, and an overall operating budget of thirty dollars for everything else. When the house opened, there were fifteen children in residence.

Thanks to the efforts of local donors and volunteers, the orphanage prevailed despite having such a tight budget. Every bit of charity helped. A local doctor, Dr. Honsberger, offered his services for free. Another man, a shoemaker named Mr. Thomas, offered free shoe repair. In 1904 the orphanage had a telephone installed and Bell Telephone gave the institution an annual donation that effectively cut the payments for it in half. That year, the annual income of the orphanage was $1,100, and after expenses there was a balance of $386. Without the supports and gifts in kind, the orphanage would have been very hard pressed to survive, let alone serve the children that it did.

By 1901, just five years after opening, it was estimated that at least a hundred children had been given shelter at the orphanage. In 1908 the statistics indicated that 107 had been admitted over time; 80 of the children had left the orphanage, and 30 remained. Two children were reported as having died during those twelve years (which was decidedly better than the statistics for children who had been housed at the Waterloo County House of Industry and Refuge).

Unmarried and childless, Mary devoted her time and life to the orphanage. She was given the opportunity to care for a baby, however, when, one morning in 1904, a basket containing a newborn boy was left on the front steps. Mary doted on him, consoling him when he cried. She would later tell him that when he cried she would carry him to her own room to care for him. Eventually, Mary adopted him and named him James Edward. Known as Edward, he was well cared for. Mary saw to it that he received a good education. She bestowed love on her adopted son, and as Edward grew up, his love for Mary equaled that of her devotion to him.

Mary was an active member of the Berlin Mennonite Church (today First Mennonite, located on the corner of King and Stirling Avenue), which assisted and supported the orphanage in many ways. The Ladies' Aid group of the church often brought food and clothing for the residents. As part of this group, Mary served her church, community, and the orphanage in other capacities, as well. In 1927 Mary, then aged sixty-five, resigned from her position as the Kitchener Orphanage Matron and bought a house nearby. Edward got married at age twenty-four, but just a few months later his appendix ruptured. He died a few days later, from peritonitis. Mary was devastated. She died on February 23, 1930, the day of Edward's funeral.

The orphanage operated in its original location for more than twenty years before it outgrew its facility. At first, an eleven-acre property was purchased on Sheldon Avenue but, due to a conflict with the YMCA, it was decided that another property needed to be found. The searchers settled for a location in Kitchener on Francis and Water Streets. By 1938, after they had moved to a location on Charles Street in Kitchener, they were ready to move again. The current location had become dilapidated and was in need of expensive repairs. A suitable property was found, whose owner had recently died. That beautiful nine-acre property, at 22 Willow Street in Waterloo, was one of the former Joseph Seagram residences. The house had sixty-five rooms.

There was a poignant connection in this choice — Joseph Seagram (and his brother Edward) had been orphaned as teens themselves, and had lived at a boys' boarding school for six years.

The property was purchased for ten thousand dollars, an amount that was reduced by two hundred dollars when a 112-foot frontage was severed to be retained by the estate. This frontage became the source of great controversy, one that involved money — tax revenue, to be exact.

While it was owned by the Seagram family, the family had paid the town of Waterloo taxes on the Willow Street property. But Waterloo's mayor was upset about the potential tax revenue loss that would result if the property was sold to a charity, which would not be required to pay taxes on it. Despite the mayor's misgivings, the orphanage purchased the property. The process was a lengthy one, however, and while negotiations (and complaints) were being dealt with, the children were split between the two buildings — ten children were relocated to Willow Street, while fifteen were still at Charles Street.

Complaints about a number things, including the potential revenue loss, caused the orphanage board to re-examine the terms of the purchase agreement. A Willow Street neighbour petitioned to have all the houses that abutted onto Willow Street, including the orphanage, declared residential properties, which would require their owners to pay tax. Rubber Industrialist A.R. Kaufman, who volunteered his services on behalf of the orphanage, renegotiated the sale of the property with the Seagram estate and, on a technicality, severed a strip of property frontage, to be retained by the Seagram interests. This severance not only resulted in a slight decrease in the cost of the property, it also changed the lay of the Willow Street land, literally speaking. As a result of the severance of the property, the narrow strip of land that fronted on Willow Street remained residential, and was owned by the Seagram estate, not the orphanage. The orphanage property was left with a very small front lawn, but most of its acreage remained in the back. The move enraged the town council, but Kaufman's strategy paid off. The rest of the children moved into what was eventually renamed Willow Hall (in order to lessen the stigma associated with the term *orphanage*).

By 1939 Willow Hall had a new matron. Miss Lydia Dankert, a Hanover woman, took over from Mary Snyder's replacement, Miss Emma Good. Miss Dankert's salary was fifty dollars per month.

Not all of the children who entered into the orphanage were orphans. Sometimes, the children had been removed from neglectful and violent homes; in other cases, the parents of the children had fallen on hard times and couldn't care for the children themselves so they committed them to the care of the orphanage. Regardless of their origins, most of the children in Willow Hall seemed to find their experience there a positive one. In the remembrances of former residents, the common thread appears to be relatively fond memories. It seems that the children enjoyed a sense of freedom but always were taken care of, had food to eat (the rations may have been meagre, but it seems they were always enough to fill hungry stomachs), and although they may not have had the best clothes or the latest toys, many recounted the good times and what they were grateful for — simple Christmas celebrations; donations of ice cream that provided unlimited eating, as it wouldn't keep; and the opportunity to make a bit of pocket money at odd jobs.

The benefits provided by the home become clear when they are contrasted with the lives of children who lived outside it. The story of one boy provides a clear example: He left the home rather abruptly when his errant mother turned back up, pleading with him to come and live with her in Toronto. He said the happiness he felt on going back to live with his mother again was short-lived when it became obvious that she was not equipped to be a parent. She had a partner who drank a lot and with whom he didn't get along. Later, he admitted that his best childhood memories were those from the Hall, which offered him a safe and comfortable home when he was at his most vulnerable. Other former residents expressed how they left Willow Hall to go on to have stable marriages and families of their own, and how they were also grateful for their time spent there.

Willow Hall closed in 1960.

THE COOMBE

The accounts from Willow Hall are very different from some of the records I reviewed about the Coombe Orphanage in Hespeler. Here children worked hard, and the place, in the memories of those who spent time there, was often harsh.

The Coombe was founded in 1905 in the former house of the town's eponymous founding father, Jacob Hespeler, who died in 1881. Initially, the Coombe was operated by Smyly Homes of Dublin as a home for relocated Irish orphans. In 1917 it was purchased by the Children's Aid Society, which operated it until 1947. In 2000 author Paul Langan wrote a booklet, *Hespeler's Hidden Secret: The Coombe Orphanage 1905–1947*, that detailed some of the harsh lives that children endured over the years while in care (confinement) at the Coombe. Documented in pictures are the children at work, doing hard manual labour for very little compensation. One former resident likened it to having to perform "slave labour."

Children under the age of fourteen were to receive board, clothing, and schooling, while those over fourteen were hired out based on their ability to perform and their perceived "worth." The rules claimed that no

The Coombe Orphanage.

intemperate or abusive families were to receive any of the children "hired out," and yet many adult survivors spoke only about relentless beatings, verbal abuse, and ill-treatment in their placements. The inspectors from the Coombe were required to visit the placements annually (but let's face it, a lot can happen in between visits and, apparently, it did). Children would either stay on the farm at the Coombe and work, or be "let out" to work at another farm. Either way, supervision for those children was still the responsibility of the Coombe superintendents. The superintendents were required to report any abuse to the Children's Aid Society, their employers. Too often, it seems, the staff at the Coombe didn't do anything.

Over the years, there were various superintendents, some who were kind to the residents, and of these there are fond memories. Others were more discipline-oriented, like Mr. Art Young, who became superintendent in 1943. Mr. Young was eventually fired by the Children's Aid Society for using excessive force against the children in his care. He had been reported to the society after a schoolteacher saw welts on a child that had been placed there by Young in a public beating for bedwetting.

In 1947 the Coombe was purchased by the Lutheran Church and ceased operation. By 1950 the building had been sold again, and was converted into rental apartments.

* * *

By the late 1800s organizations for orphaned children in Ireland, Scotland, and throughout the United Kingdom were unable to accommodate all of the children coming into their care. One of the solutions was to send orphaned children overseas to Canadian receiving homes. Of these organizations, some of the more prominent ones were Smyly's, Barnardo's, the Bristol Emigration Society, and the Painswick Emigration Home. Over the years, under the auspices of these and other organizations, thousands of orphaned and vulnerable children made the journey to Canada, not knowing where they were heading or what would befall them when they got there. Many started their voyage with siblings but ended up separated and sent to different homes. Some lost track of their families and never saw them again.

It has been estimated that between 1870 and 1957 a hundred thousand children were relocated to Canada by these agencies — seventy thousand of them arrived in Ontario, alone. They were sent by organizations that were predominately faith-based charities, not to find adoptive families but to fill shortages in the rural labour force on farms and in agricultural communities. By 1897 Ontario legislated regulations to monitor these relocation agencies. Ultimately, supervision for these children fell upon the newly created Children's Aid Societies.

For many of these marginalized and otherwise destitute children, life abroad in Canada was considered to be better than what they had come from, since many had escaped untold poverty and neglect. For some residents of the Coombe, it was the first time that they had had a stable home in their lives; for others, depending upon the superintendent in charge or their placement, life was hell.

Today, an estimated 12 percent of Canadians can trace their ancestry to a British Home Child.

PART THREE

Dodgy Dealings and Risky Business

8

BOOTLEGGERS, JOSEPH SEAGRAM, AND AL CAPONE

> I am like any other man. All I do is supply a demand.
>
> — Al Capone

WHILE WORKING IN THE PUBLIC HISTORY FIELD, I have often been asked by people apparently seeking an inside scoop, "Did Mennonites back in the day drink alcohol?" My response is a quick one that seems to surprise many of the askers: "Yes. Yes they did, and they often made it."

The discouragement of alcohol use among Mennonites is a relatively recent phenomenon. In fact, at the end of the sixteenth century, there were many successful Mennonite distilleries in Europe. Successful distillery businesses continued in North America following the group's emigration to Pennsylvania and eventually their migration to Waterloo County. Today, the use of alcohol by Mennonites varies from group to group.

Mennonites living in early Waterloo County (at least 150 years ago) were very familiar with the process of fermentation, and many engaged in winemaking and brewing beer at home. Many farms also had small-scale stills that made whisky. (In fact, at one time it was the custom for a farmer to pay his labourers a portion of home-distilled spirits along with their wages).

Apple orchards were ubiquitous — every farm had one. The bounty these offered allowed farmers to produce alcohol — as one way to preserve the harvest. Fresh, sweet apple cider quickly transforms (ferments) into hard (alcoholic) apple cider.

Sometimes the apple cider froze and a thick beverage emerged — a favourite Waterloo County drink called "Apple Jack." Apple Jack is a liqueur-type product, produced not unlike icewine is today. Freezing the cider allowed the sugars to break down even more, and the result was a thick, sweet, and very potent apple-flavoured liqueur. In the nineteenth century this drink was enjoyed by everyone. Children were often given alcoholic beverages if water sources were suspect. (Keep in mind that at the time most livestock roamed freely, which also meant that watercourses could become polluted with feces. In addition, with the establishment of factories along the Grand River, and especially tributary Schneider's Creek, industrial pollution also contributed to tainted water sources. Although the fermentation and distillation of liquids offers no protection against chemical waste, it will destroy bacterial pathogens, making alcohol a safer choice to imbibe.)

Alcohol production also provided business opportunities. Farming was a full-time job, but its proceeds were not always consistent, particularly in the winter months, and so, many men had a secondary source of income. When the first grist mills (for grinding grain) appeared in Waterloo County, there was also the lucrative potential for distilling.

In 1816 Joseph Schneider, whose land bordered on the swampy area of what is now Kitchener's Victoria Park, erected a saw mill. Many of his neighbours planted large orchards and set up cider mills instead.

One man, known as "Indian Sam" Eby, was, among other things, a distiller of whisky. He was a controversial character. He received the nickname "Indian Sam" because of his close but complex relationship to the Indigenous Peoples in the Waterloo County area. Although he sold alcohol to them (and to his neighbours), he was more than just a businessman. Eby acted as a translator for the Mississaugas and would also minister to them. In 1804 he established a distillery business at a crossroads, where he traded whisky in exchange for the Mississaugas' furs. By 1808 fellow settlers began to complain that Eby's actions had caused numerous problems in the relations between the Indigenous Peoples and the Mennonite settlers. Eventually, many of the Mississaugas gave up the use of liquor altogether and converted to Methodism. In 1833 one German immigrant to Waterloo remarked that the Indigenous people he had met were "the most peaceable people, a large number of them Christians."

It is no surprise that mills in one form or another became some of the first types of commercial ventures built in this area. Waterloo County was known for its good (and plentiful) sources of water, the key source of power for mill operations. Overshot waterwheels drove the huge grindstones that ground the wheat, barley, and rye used to make liquor. For farmers, the mills were also social centres. As historian Elizabeth Bloomfield puts it in *Waterloo Township Through Two Centuries*:

> [A] trip to the mill was often a matter of two or three days and comfortable, where he [the farmer who brought his grain to be ground] met the other farmers, so that it became a social centre, and a business mart as well. They warmed their victuals and made coffee at the fireplace and slept on the floor or on the bags of bran.

Abraham Erb, an early Mennonite miller, installed a large fireplace and wooden floor in his grist mill; there farmers could spend time while waiting. Because there were no hotels in the area yet, Erb outfitted the basement of his mill with rough furniture so that some of the farmers who had travelled a great distance could stay in relative comfort overnight before undertaking their long journey home.

Waterloo eventually became famous for its production of alcohol. Indeed, distilled liquor has been one of the most successful and famous locally produced products (particularly those distilled under the name of Seagram). Brewing beer has been equally successful. There are still those who remember the smells of Waterloo's Kuntz Brewery when the wind was right and the brewing was in full swing.

In 1857 William Hespeler, a merchant, and George Randall, a contractor, built a small distillery known as the Waterloo Distillery. Though it may sound strange, the business also included a dry goods store. It was near the corner of King and Erb Streets in Waterloo. By 1863 Hespeler and Randall took in another partner, William Roos. The next year, history was made with the hiring of a young man by the name of Joseph Emm Seagram.

In 1870 Seagram managed to buy out Hespeler's interests. With the change in ownership, the name of the company changed also, becoming George Randall and Company — Seagram had yet to add his name to the operation. That changed in 1878, when enterprising Seagram bought out Randall. Seagram and his remaining partner William Roos operated as "Randall and Company" until 1881, when they officially changed the name of the company to "Seagram and Roos."

Ever the entrepreneur, Seagram bought out Roos in 1884 and became the sole proprietor. It was at this time that he tweaked the identity of his business, operating it under two different names: Joseph Seagram Flour Mill and Distillery Company and Joseph E. Seagram, Miller, Distiller. Why he chose to do this is unclear. Seagram incorporated the company in 1911, finally changing the name to the familiar Joseph E. Seagram and Sons, Limited. By the time Seagram died in 1919, the business empire he had built, including the Waterloo distillery, had evolved into a major exporting company and his brand names were widely known — particularly in the United States.

There were those who eschewed the use of alcohol, claiming it caused no end of problems for families. The temperance movement, as it was known, had been alive and well in Waterloo County throughout the nineteenth century, long before its return in the twentieth. For example, Joseph E. Schneider (son of pioneer Joseph Schneider), who eventually took over the operation of the family farm, was a temperance man. He rented some of the family land in the 1840s and '50s to itinerant preachers who held revival and temperance meetings in large tents in the area that today houses St. Paul's Lutheran Church. These meetings were well attended and well organized. In time, the meetings were instrumental in helping to sway some of the Mennonites' feelings toward total abstinence from alcohol. By the twentieth century, many Mennonites had chosen to abstain altogether, although the attitude regarding the potential evils of alcohol were complex and, as stated at the beginning of this chapter, varied from group to group. This lack of uniformity was fostered by the *Canada Temperance Act* (1878), which let individual communities decide whether or not they wanted to ban the sale of alcohol. Those that chose to ban it became known as "local option" communities. For those that didn't, like Waterloo, alcohol production, distillation, and distribution continued virtually unimpeded. That is, until "Prohibition."

Following the end of the First World War, and just after Joseph Seagram died, the United States brought in the Eighteenth Amendment to the Constitution, popularly known as Prohibition. Immediately after the ban on alcohol sales in the United States, at the beginning of 1920, the smuggling of alcohol became big business — in both the United States and Canada. North of the U.S. border, Canadian laws allowed a bit more lenience in production and sales. The *Canada Temperance Act* permitted the making of alcohol but restricted where, how, and by whom it could be sold or exported.

With Joseph Seagram gone, his sons took over the business. The generational shift at the company was accompanied by a significant change in the way it was run. Rumours flew that illegal shipments of alcohol were being smuggled out of the Seagram's plant on a daily basis. One local policeman, Ephraim Zinkann (the local "Elliott Ness"), raided a private house on Homewood Avenue in Kitchener that had been rumoured to be selling bootlegged Seagram whisky. There was a fight, and bullets flew during the raid. In the end, Ephraim Zinkann confiscated fifty-three cases of whisky and forty-five ten-gallon kegs of rye. This was a significant coup for the police, who were a bit shorthanded in their efforts to enforce the alcohol control law in Waterloo County. (The same was true elsewhere in the province).

An account from the diary of one Allan Buehler provides a real eye-opener. It provides a first-hand view of alcohol smuggling in Waterloo at the time, showing just how successful it was and how connected it was to those wanting to smuggle alcohol into the United States.

Allan was an Old Order Mennonite, and at one point during Prohibition, he worked for smugglers purported to be working for Al Capone! In his 1977 memoir, Buehler revealed something that, as they say, blew the cover off the pot. During the Prohibition era in the United

States, Buehler was working nights at the Heppler and Sehl garage. (That building still stands, in Uptown Waterloo, redeveloped as a local watering hole known as the Night School Bar, which caters to the seasonal university student population.)

In Buehler's time, many cars would come and go from the garage: it was a very busy place. Some of these were patrons staying at the Kent Hotel (today the Heuther) who parked their cars overnight at the garage. They would request to have their gas tanks topped up and the car delivered to them the next day. On occasion, even the Seagram family cars could be found there, waiting to be picked up by the chauffeur.

Buehler revealed that bootleggers from Windsor-Detroit had sequestered a section of the Heppler and Sehl's downstairs and turned it into their headquarters — and that these bootleggers were none other than a branch of the Al Capone gang. According to Buehler, four Reo trucks were kept gassed up and ready to go at all times. He said the gang leader drove a large Cadillac car with bulletproof glass. Sometimes, when someone was placing an order, Buehler said, he would answer the phone call and pass along coded messages to the bootleggers directly.

Buehler describes the highly sophisticated system used to smuggle liquor. The business was large and well organized. It did not sell locally, choosing instead to export everything. He said that bootleggers from all over Ontario came to the garage for their supplies — always at night. He called them "professional gangsters who carried revolvers." Buehler said that the gangsters employed "spotters" at various locations throughout Waterloo, who kept on the look-out for potential raids by the Ontario Provincial Police (the OPP).

While it was legal to produce alcohol in Canada, selling it was more restricted, and in some ways the various provincial laws were ambiguous. Bootleggers saw an opportunity for profit. Canadian law dictated that it was legal to export alcohol, but not to countries that were under prohibition — like the United States (whose laws differed somewhat from state to state, making things also complicated there). Further, there were excise taxes to be paid on exports from Canada. Bootleggers wanted to avoid both the Canadian excise taxes and the export restriction to the United States Inspectors hired by the government were assigned to watch for infractions, but in some areas it was the police — in Ontario, the OPP — who enforced the law. In order to avoid running into them, the gangsters would go to Seagram's distillery after midnight to load up their boozy cargo. They would then drive along the back streets of Waterloo, never using the same route twice, and head for Elmira. Buehler said that there was a warehouse somewhere near Elmira, where they would hide the whisky and then drive the trucks back to the garage (he did not disclose where the warehouse was, or if he even knew its exact location).

The gang would usually be able to evade the police, but occasionally they were spotted and the chase was on. According to Buehler, the smugglers would try to outrace the police, but if they were caught, they would show their export papers, then innocently drive on to Toronto or Hamilton (rather than to the Elmira-area warehouse) to export the load in question, and there was nothing the police could do about it — because exporting alcohol was legal. There were occasional gun fights when police chased them, Buehler said, and sometimes trucks would return to the garage with bullet holes in the back and sides.

In his memoir, Buehler describes how he, himself, got caught up in the drinking involved in the illegal liquor trade. He tells of how he would sometimes go to the local bars to deliver cook cheese, a Mennonite favourite. On occasion, when customers from the garage recognized him, they would buy him drinks as a courtesy. According to Buehler, by the time he had delivered to three hotels he was "pretty well loaded." At the time, "a person was not considered drunk as long as he could navigate by himself; he was considered drunk when he could no longer walk by himself." Buehler continues, "If this was the definition of being drunk, then I guess I was not drunk, but I sure was loaded."

The temptation to become involved in alcohol smuggling would have been difficult to resist for a young man, strict Mennonite upbringing or no. Allan would have been making a very lucrative living (and arguably leading a very exciting life) for a rural lad at a time when well-paying jobs like his were in relatively short supply — regardless of the fringe benefits.

Buehler is very clear that, although he only had to open and close doors, he knew very well what was going on and should not, according to his Old Order Mennonite beliefs and upbringing, have been a part of any of it. It is evident that Buehler felt a lot of guilt and regret for his involvement.

The Seagram family eventually, in 1928, sold their interests in the family business to the Bronfman family. The Bronfmans had come to Canada in 1889 after fleeing anti-Semitism in Russia. They began their empire in the hotel business, owning three hotels in Winnipeg by the middle of the First World War.

In 1924 Samuel Bronfman opened his first distillery in Quebec and incorporated it under the name Distillers Corporation Limited. Around 1927 Joseph E. Seagram & Sons Ltd. (now under the management of Joseph's sons) sold their shares and took the company public. The Distillers Corporation (the Bronfmans) acquired all of the stock in the Seagram business and, as a public company, formed Distillers Corporation-Seagram's Ltd.

Their company continued to grow and prosper throughout the 1920s until around 1933, mostly through their exportation of Canadian alcohol into the United States. Before 1930 it was legal under Canadian law to sell alcohol to American buyers, but after 1930 it became illegal to sell or export alcohol to any county that was observing Prohibition. To get around this obstacle, companies like Seagram's would, quite legally, export their alcohol to St. Pierre and Miquelon, self-governing French territories south of Newfoundland. Here, the alcohol was stored and then illegally transported by smugglers to U.S. customers. By 1933 American Prohibition had ended; however, the RCMP had already launched an investigation into illegal liquor smuggling, and in 1934 Abraham, Allan, Harry, and Samuel Bronfman were arrested. Their case was dismissed in 1935.

Local stories and urban legends are replete with bootlegging escapades that involve at least two local hotels: the Huether and the Walper. It was a poorly kept secret that during Canada's brief period of prohibition that followed the First World War (1918 to 1920), many hotels kept secret bars — speakeasies — that were most often hidden in their basements; although there few locally that were located off the premises, as well. It has been rumoured that Seagram built a private railroad to transport liquor to the Huether from his distillery. It was said that there was a cold room that smugglers used to store beer.

In discussions of Prohibition, imagination is never in short supply. While conducting routine maintenance in 1961, the Waterloo Works Department found a big hole under the road on a property adjacent to the hotel, and in so doing revealed an old cavern and tunnel that had been excavated on the western side of the hotel. Many have speculated about their origin and use, but most historians believe the cavern probably dates from the late nineteenth century and that it had nothing to do with gangsters or Prohibition. Other renovation work in 1981 has revealed the foundations for a former malt house, as well.

Any speakeasies in operation during Prohibition would have had limited bottles of alcohol on hand, for security reasons, and there would have been a watchman keeping an eye over who came or went. To get in, you needed to be a familiar face. If the police were threatening to attempt entry, there were safeguards — special chutes in false walls allowed bartenders to throw liquor bottles and glasses down, and hidden water hoses were kept on hand to wash the debris away. If the police wanted to lay charges, they would have to be able to produce at least a minimal amount — at least several ounces — of liquor; if there was no evidence, no charges could be laid. Suspicions didn't count. Hiding the liquor available for sale (or already sold) was a fact of life for speakeasies. Some had a tougher time of it than others, though. It was said that the Walper not only sold illegal liquor during Prohibition but that it actually distilled it in the basement in a hidden room. Once distilled, it was supposedly smuggled out through underground tunnels. So goes another local legend, anyway.

David Kuntz and his brother Jacob came to the Doon area in the 1830s as immigrants from Germany. After working for a few years as barrel makers, they moved to Waterloo. Their first involvement in brewing originated on Princess Street in the former Wilhelm Rebscher's brewery (today the site of the Huether Hotel). They built a malt house near Erb and Regina behind what was then Bowman's Hotel. They were enterprising young men, accredited with having made the barrels that contained their beer as well as the wheelbarrow in which they delivered it. One account states that David even made the bricks that they used to build their brewery.

A full brewery was constructed in the early 1860s at King and William Streets, and by 1865 the Kuntzes were using hops and barley that they had grown to brew their beer. Because of the high quality of the water they were using, which came from a nearby spring, they initially named their business the Kuntz Spring Brewery.

David moved for some time to Hamilton to set up another brewing business, turning his first business over to his son, Louis. He returned to Waterloo after several years and served on the town council in 1876. Sadly, in 1891 Louis died at the young age of thirty-nine following complications from an appendectomy (presumably from infection). David Kuntz died a year later. Louis's son took over the struggling business in 1910, and following his own untimely death at age thirty-eight during the First World War, his brothers stepped in, selling the firm in 1929 to E.P. Taylor.

Taylor changed the name from Kuntz Breweries to Kuntz-Carling, and, following the Second World War, to just Carling Brewery. The business, still located at King and William Streets, near the original spring, was later known as Carling-O'Keefe and then Labatt's. It was from this location that older locals remember the once-familiar malting smell, now long since gone with Uptown Waterloo development.

During Prohibition, policemen like Ephraim Zinkann struggled to combat the illegal smuggling of Seagram's whisky and Kuntz's beer. The two firms were big employers in the area, and they were both rumoured to be supplying customers beyond local boundaries. It was said that the brewery was selling whole boxcar loads of beer right out of the backdoor docking area, but police had a hard time trying to keep up with the bootleggers. Empty trucks acted as decoys to throw police off the scent. Making matters more difficult for those trying to enforce the law was the fact that, since Waterloo was still a small town, there were only two police officers assigned to patrol the smuggling operations. Still, sometimes they got lucky. From time to time, large amounts of illegal beer and whisky caches were seized from barns and homes around Kitchener-Waterloo, even though both Seagram's and Kuntz's apparently continued illegal operations throughout the Prohibition era.

The brewery was finally demolished in 1993.

* * *

There are many other interesting tales to be told of the Prohibition era. By manipulating the many legal loopholes in legislation, distilleries and breweries were able to increase the ways in which they sold their wares. In the Waterloo Region, residents could get a doctor's prescription for the medicinal or "home use" of alcohol, and both Seagram's and Kuntz used mail-order businesses based in Quebec to get around local bans. Locals could send money to a Montreal address and in return receive Waterloo-brewed beer or whisky delivered right to their front door — legally. The necessity for this ended in 1927, when people could once again legally buy their alcohol, now from government outlets run by the Liquor Control Board of Ontario — the LCBO.

9

BODYSNATCHING FOR PROFIT

> None but those who have experienced them can conceive of the enticements of science.
>
> — Mary Wollstonecraft Shelley, *Frankenstein*, 1818

IT IS ONE THING TO WILL YOUR BODY to science and quite another to have that choice made for you. In 1850s Waterloo County, there was no such thing as a donor card. There was, however, Dr. Christ (pronounced *Krisst*). Christ presented himself publicly as a medical doctor who, during the day at least, performed his duties as a physician, seeing patients in his rented office space above a furniture factory in Waterloo ("on the road to Bridgeport"). Dr. Christ lived an unusual kind of marginal existence, operating in secret under the cover of darkness, in a nefarious business for profit. Dr. Christ was a bodysnatcher, and his victims, the recently dead, couldn't argue back with him.

* * *

Bodysnatching has gone on for centuries, if not millennia. Although the act of bodysnatching provokes societal disgust and criminal consequences for those engaged in it, it must be said that the bodies obtained have made an important contribution to medical science. It may come as a bit of a shock, but a lot of what we know today about anatomy and the medical processes within the body has actually grown from the study of corpses — mostly illegally obtained corpses — in centuries past.

As early as the fifteenth and sixteenth centuries, medical students were actually encouraged by their professors to "obtain corpses of their own" on which to practise their skills and from which to grow their knowledge in the field of anatomical dissection. Of course, their professors did not provide directions as to how the students might get the corpses (because of the obvious legal implications). Some medical students got busy on their own and, yes, removed corpses of the recently dead themselves. Others purchased them from body sellers, who had snatched the corpses of criminals, the diseased, and the poor who had been buried in potter's fields. Bodysnatching was a highly lucrative business, though it was a largely invisible one since neither the body thief nor the body purchaser wanted to be identifiable. Those whose bodies were stolen were often unidentifiable, too, since most represented the lowest of the low — the poor and forgotten. In death, they, too, were mostly anonymous. Sadly, most were worth more in death than they were alive.

One side note: bodysnatching should not to be confused with grave-robbing, which carries its own stigma and set of perceived social, religious, and criminal implications. Bodysnatching is best defined as the unauthorized removal of a corpse from its burial site. Grave-robbing is the act of looting a grave for the goods that have been buried with the dead. In general, there is little grave-robbing — at least in comparison to bodysnatching. This is not the case at archaeological sites, however. At such sites, it is almost always the artifacts that are of interest to those digging.

Recently, there has been significant debate about archaeological practices, since the artifacts that have been retrieved — material such as statuaries, gold jewellery, etc. — have often come from graves. The removal of mummies from the pyramids, for example, was most often related to the theft of the sarcophagi that housed them. Today there is legislation in the United States to repatriate Indigenous goods and skeletons (biomaterial) to their rightful tribal stakeholders and heirs. The *Native American Graves Protection and Repatriation Act* (NAGPRA), is a United States federal law enacted on November 16, 1990, that ensures such repatriation. In Canada, the practice of Indigenous goods repatriation is not yet legislated. Currently, First Nations' grave goods, artifacts, and skeletal remains are returned by archives, museums, etc., on a discretionary basis to the appropriate stakeholders.

Prior to the *Anatomy Act 1832*, the only legally sourced supply of medical dissection corpses in the United Kingdom were those who had been condemned to "death and dissection" in court. For those who engaged in the practice of bodysnatching, a new term emerged, *resurrectionists* or *resurrection men*. The use of the latter term should not imply that women were not involved as bodysnatchers — they were. But more often, rather than digging up the graves, they would act as lookouts or would arrange the purchase and sales of the corpses.

Before 1832 the act of "interfering with a grave" was considered to be a summary offence (in the United States it is known as a misdemeanor). This meant that punishment would most likely be a fine. This would change in time, but even when the punishment increased, the trade was so lucrative that any perceived punishment paled in comparison to the potential profit. In fact, bodysnatching became so prevalent that it was common practice for bereaved friends and family members with financial means to find ingenious ways to protect the graves of their loved ones, thereby initiating another lucrative business — grave securities. Traditionally produced wooden coffins were replaced by iron ones. In other cases, iron framework bars or "mortsafes" would be built over the top of a burial plot to deter any interference with the grave beneath it.

Other remedies were quite ingenious. One example featured exploding coffins that contained guns or "grave torpedoes" that would detonate if anyone attempted to open them. Ironically, as the protection of graves became more commonplace, so, too, did the growing fear of being buried alive. Technology was applied to the existing security, and soon patents began to appear for coffin alarm systems that could be used if someone awoke inside a coffin. At this, a saying comes to mind — saved by the bell. At one time, people were sometimes buried with a bell that they could ring in case of an emergency (which is what I would call being buried alive). An 1834 account describes an incident in which a man awoke inside his coffin and rang the bell beside him. As historical irony would have it, the man was indeed rescued … by a bodysnatcher who was working nearby.

The idea of "resurrecting" the dead to repurpose them was so common in the early nineteenth century that it crossed into the popular literature of its day. In 1818, a familiar novel written by Mary Wollstonecraft Shelley — namely, *Frankenstein* — was published. It was conceived and written during the stormy summer of 1816, a weather event that can be traced to one of the most powerful volcanic eruptions to ever take place: the eruption of Mount Tambora in Indonesia in 1815. This eruption was so violent that its ash spread virtually everywhere throughout the world, triggering extreme weather that significantly lowered temperatures on a global scale. This caused widespread crop failures for the next several years and, not surprisingly, food shortages for both humans and their livestock. Yellowed sunsets became the norm as the ash lingered in the skies for months.

A year later, weather patterns were still being affected and with life-threatening consequences. The year 1816 became known as the "Year Without a Summer" because even the normally temperate months of the year were impacted by extensive frosts that destroyed field crops and food sources. (This is also referred to as a volcanic winter.) In Waterloo County, Mennonite farmers reported that they found it difficult to feed their animals and themselves as their own crops failed. It was said that many resorted to gleaning the grasses from along the banks of the Grand River in order to feed their animals. (It is interesting that many early local buildings date from this time. Joseph Schneider Haus National Historic Site and the Abraham Erb Grist Mill, for example, were each built in about 1816.) It would seem that the Mennonite survivors did not passively wait for the bad weather to pass over.

In 1816 Wollstonecraft (then nineteen and unmarried) and her lover (and later husband), Percy Bysshe Shelley, visited their friend and fellow writer Lord Byron in Switzerland. Byron was holed up in a rented villa along Lake Geneva. Entertaining his guests was increasingly difficult because of the miserable weather, which precluded any thought of outdoor excursions. The three often sat up long into the night, entertaining themselves by telling ghost stories. At one point, they decided that they would each go off alone and write a story that they would come back to share. Mary's story hints at the current events, or tabloid news, of the day — involving resurrectionism and "rebirth," with consequences — the story we know today as *Frankenstein*.

Bodysnatching was a common practice throughout the world, although the reasons for its prevalence (and consequences) varied by culture and geography. In Canada, medical students frequently found it difficult to obtain fresh corpses, in part because of the lack of means of preservation. This was before the practice of embalming became common and before the invention of refrigeration. In many cases, students had to take the matter into their own hands, and found themselves resorting to the practice of bodysnatching. For this, local epidemics provided unexpected opportunities.

During the winter of 1875, for example, typhoid fever struck a convent school in Montreal, and many of the corpses were stolen by bodysnatchers before bereaved relatives arrived to claim their dead. Medical students at McGill University were documented as "resurrecting" the dead for two reasons: one, to further their own knowledge and practice of dissection; and two, to supply the dissection needs of their professors. For the latter, the students often received a payment of thirty to fifty dollars per body (an effective and lucrative method of paying for tuition, to be sure). The students often worked in the winter, because the frozen ground delayed the digging of graves and burial. Bodies were often laid out above-ground in "dead houses" until the spring thaw, making them easier to steal.

In Ontario the *Toronto Globe* reported in the 1850s that it was unnecessary to procure corpses for dissection "as plenty can be procured in a legitimate way." In 1843 the Province of Canada (as Ontario and Quebec were then known) passed an anatomy act that stated that anyone who died destitute in a provincially funded hospital or poorhouse would have his (or her) body collected by a local inspector, whose responsibility it would be to deliver said corpse to a medical school, which would then be responsible for keeping records of receipt and providing appropriate burial practices upon completion of any anatomical use of the bodies.

A year after the *Globe*'s declaration, an anonymous doctor wrote to the paper to say that, as the number of medical schools grew, bringing more students and their study needs, bodysnatching would increase at a proportional rate. He was right. For some decades after 1850, the number of people who died in provincially funded institutions was not sufficient to meet the demands of the medical schools.

And so, once again, to Dr. Friedrich (Frederick) Christ. The scenario sketched by the "anonymous doctor's" letter to the *Globe* makes me wonder if the doctor in question knew something personally about the business of bodysnatching, or had inside knowledge of the supply and demand of the trade. In other words, I have wondered if the letter's author was Dr. Christ himself.

The dead provided other means for those not too fussy about how they made a buck to supplement their income — namely, complete skeletons. Once a cadaver had been processed (freed) of its flesh, a skeleton could travel anywhere with no smell or decay, which would have been an advantage for someone buying one from a supplier who was far away. In Waterloo County, apparently, Dr. Christ was the supplier.

Dr. Frederick Christ arrived in Waterloo in 1853 as an immigrant from Mecklinberg, Germany, and opened his new practice in the office of a local newspaper in Waterloo. The newspaper was a popular German-language paper, owned by a future mayor of the town of Waterloo (Moses Springer).

Christ first advertised his services through an ad of introduction on December 1, 1853, in another German-language paper, *Der Deutsche Canadier*. Two weeks later, on January 12, 1854, a more formal ad appeared in the same paper:

> Dr. F. Christ, Physician, Surgeon and Accoucher[24] introduces himself to his German fellow countrymen to assist in all matters of medical science. My residence is with Mr.

> Teuscher, Editor of the "*Canadischen Bauernfreundes*" above Clark & Co.'s furniture factory on the road to Bridgeport.

In another ad, Christ mentions that he would make weekly visits to "Mr. Nicholas Hug's Inn," located in New Germany (Maryhill), which was settled by predominately German-speaking immigrants, particularly from 1830 to the 1850s. Few records of Christ's medical expertise exist apart from one reference, a thank-you notice in one of the local papers from the family of a recently deceased consumptive. In its expression of gratitude, the family praised Christ for his "unremitting solicitude and devotion" in his treatment of the patient.

It would seem that this was a rare commendation of the doctor's skills or behaviour, as he was often embroiled in local spats and controversies (even before his later actions came to light). Christ was known to be quite vocal in his opinions concerning religion and politics, particularly when he had been over-imbibing at a local tavern. These opinions were not widely appreciated by his new neighbours. It is likely that his strong and offensive opinions, and his vehemence in expressing them, impaired his ability to build a healthy practice. In any event, things did not go well financially for Dr. Christ. Nor, it seems, did things go well for him legally, and just several years after opening his new practice Dr. Christ found himself on the wrong side of the law. In fact, he was twice listed as being "a prisoner" in the Berlin Gaol — once in 1856 and again in 1859.

Lack of money continued to dog him, but soon Dr. Christ found a gruesome way to supplement his meagre earnings.[25] In his endeavour he employed an Elmira man, Hugo Werthman, a furrier by trade, to assist him. Dr. Christ and his partner, under cover of darkness, visited local cemeteries to obtain recently buried remains for their stock in trade. Presumably, Werthman and his sons did the dirty work of digging up the remains while Dr. Christ prepared the bodies, converting them into skeletons for sale by boiling them down in a big kettle in a barn behind his residence. Locals noticed the noxious smells emanating from the place, but it was Christ, himself, who the real source of his own undoing.

The money he received for his dastardly deeds was apparently so good that he began to brag about his "work." Among his numerous other failings,

Dr. Christ was particularly guilty of narcissism and pride. On occasion, he would go into a local tavern (Schnarr's Tavern), get drunk, and publicly regale other patrons with details of his business dealings, methods, and "sources of income." He even wagered money that the families of particular individuals were none the wiser for the fact that their loved ones were not located in the graves in which they had been interred. His claim? That the graves were empty because he was the one who had emptied them. At some point, the locals were finally fed up with his bragging and decided once and for all to investigate his tales. What the public was to discover was that Dr. Christ may have had a very big mouth, but he was actually and unfortunately telling the truth.

Christ and his accomplice, Mr. Werthman, were summarily arrested and prosecuted by none other than local magistrate (and newspaper owner) Moses Springer, who had become the first reeve of Waterloo in 1857 — the year that Waterloo was incorporated as a village.

On September 2, 1859, the *Berlin Telegraph,* under the headline "Resurrectionists in Waterloo," reported that Christ had been remanded for trial on a charge of grave-robbing. Moses Springer stated that he knew that Christ was in the business of preparing skeletons for sale. Christ was unrepentant, bold even, stating that he "had a right to do it and it was nobody's business how he made his money." The newspapers had a field day. The Montreal-based *Huntingdon Herald* reported,

> Berlin: A distressing investigation was held before the Magistrates of Berlin, on Wednesday, involving the character of one of the medical gentlemen of that town, another residing in Elmira, and a gentleman closely connected with the first-charged offender. It seems that for some time suspicious hints and circumstances, and smells, had indicated that the resurrection trade was being revived in Berlin, and that the remains of certain bodies had been conveyed to the premises of a medical gentleman, and, after dissection, the flesh had been consumed by boiling. The circumstances were so pointed that the magistrates deemed them sufficient to issue warrants for the arrest

> of the parties accused, and search warrants were also put into the hands of the officers to examine the Doctor's premises, and there accordingly they found the mutilated remains of several human bodies. Among these were the remains of a fine young lad named Eby, the son of Mr. Abraham Eby, of Bridgeport. The youth had been accidently killed at a soiree at Bridgeport a week or two ago, and his body interred, amid the heartfelt sorrow of a multitude of friends. A portion of his body was found on the premises of the accused, and they were sworn to by the afflicted father from certain marks. Portions of two other bodies were found, which the accused stated were those of certain persons; the tale was found to be false. The bodies appear all to have been taken from a graveyard in Berlin.

It would seem the final blow to end Dr. Christ's grisly business dealings was his theft of young Edward Eby's body. Edward was only five years old when he died. The grief and outrage arising from the tragic death of such a young victim (he was accidentally shot and mortally wounded while attending a Sunday School picnic) was heightened by the fact that Edward was the grandson of prominent early Waterloo County settler and founding father Bishop Benjamin Eby, who had, among many other community building contributions, established the church and cemetery where young Edward was laid to rest. (First Mennonite Church, as it is known today, is also the final resting place for many of the 1834 Galt cholera victims.) By publicly bragging about the theft and undignified treatment of a prominent family member, particularly one so young, Dr. Christ further debased himself, and his reputation had plummeted to a new low. There was no turning back, and, regardless of his attempts to justify and argue in support of his actions, Christ had burned all of his bridges.

The court disagreed with Christ's claims of innocence, and Christ and Werthman were summarily found guilty as charged. Their sentence? Three months in the Berlin Gaol. (Shortly after his release, Werthman was charged in Hamilton for stealing furs.)

Christ returned, at least for a time, to his practice as a doctor, but it seems that his business was no longer a viable one — and trouble followed him. He would soon become entangled in a salacious scandal regarding the death of his first wife. The gossip was that Christ was the real reason behind her death.

Dr. Christ and his wife, Emilie, had three children — two girls and one boy. His son, named Fritz after his father (Fritz is a nickname for Friedrich), was born on October 19, 1861, but died on November 10. Little Fritz was just three weeks old. It was said that the doctor and his wife were devastated. Emilie, it was rumoured, became quite depressed. In May 1866 she died at the age of forty-one following "a lingering illness." It was not the illness that caused Emilie's death, however; it was strychnine. Although her death was officially ruled a suicide, there was strong suspicion that the good doctor actually poisoned her himself. There was no solid evidence on which to arrest him, but as stated, the word about town was that many suspected Christ of having murdered his wife. His departure from the Waterloo area shortly after his wife's death only served to fan the flames of suspicion.

Christ left in September and moved to Lansing, Michigan, to start a new life and practice. It is not clear what happened to the children, as it seems that he left for the States by himself. If he arrived alone, however, he did not remain so for long — a wedding announcement on December 24, 1866, proclaimed Christ to be the proud new husband of Pauline Meyer.

They, too, had three children, but their marriage was a relatively short one. After seven years, Pauline descended into madness (became insane) and died at thirty-one in 1874 (also, suspiciously, from strychnine poisoning). Dr. Christ was reportedly heartbroken by her death; indeed, just one year later he took his own life, swallowing an overdose of morphine. The *Grand Rapids Eagle*, reporting on his death in January 21, 1875, said that after her death, he had "apparently cared little for life, indulging considerably in drink."

Christ left behind an enigmatic suicide note that simply said, "I have done the best I could to benefit mankind, but my efforts have not always been appreciated; therefore I go to join my dear wife." There were no apologies made to any of the families of his victims, nor was there any mention of any of his children. In approaching death, it appears his thoughts were only of himself.

That Christ was a bodysnatcher for profit is clear, but was he also a murderer and possibly even a narcissistic sociopath? Who can know for sure? Many bodysnatchers did their work quietly and under a cloak of secrecy. Christ was openly a braggart and seemed proudly resolute about his actions. The fact that he lost two wives under similar suspicious circumstances (and within a relatively short period of time) is mysterious. Christ may have been responsible for those deaths, but we will never know for certain. Whatever the case may be, it is sad that his sentence for the crimes for which he was convicted was such a shockingly short one — he was, after all, guilty of a great many grievous transgressions. In the end, it seems that justice was not done.

That Christ managed to serve so little time in jail as a result of his crimes, although disappointing, is not unusual. At the time, the law did not always punish bodysnatchers with stiff sentences; nor did the justice system always take their crimes as seriously as it would in years to come. However, I believe that there is more to the story. Christ's light sentence was not just a consequence of the lack of seriousness accorded the crime of bodysnatching; it was also reflective of Christ's social status.

As with those committed to the Waterloo County House of Industry and Refuge, people marginalized due to poverty, age, and other infirmities who had brushes with the law were often sentenced to be locked away — in jail or in the poorhouse — for years at a time. This punishment was extremely harsh, since many of those convicted had only been trying to survive when they engaged in the petty thefts, public begging, prostitution, etc. Christ, on the other hand, was afforded greater leniency because he was of a higher social status (and a male in a position of trust) than were the inmates of the House of Industry. Suspect as his mental state should have been, Christ was never subjected to an evaluation of his mental health. Although given a minor sentence for crimes that were too obvious to be ignored, Christ, as a member of the establishment, was able to live his life of crime relatively unmolested.

PART FOUR

In the Devil's Snare: Beyond the Veil

10

WITCHCRAFT, HEALING … AND MENNONITES?

> *Brauche* or *Braucherei*, in the "Pennsylvania Dutch" dialect … is probably still being practised in other areas of the United States and Canada where "Pennsylvania Dutch" people have settled.
>
> — David W. Kriebel, *Powwowing Among the Pennsylvania Dutch*

WAS WITCHCRAFT ALIVE AND WELL in Waterloo County? It depends upon who you ask.

Like their ancestors, many of the early Pennsylvania German settlers to Waterloo County (including the Mennonites and Amish) condoned and sought solace from folk healers commonly known as "charmers," *Brauchers* (pronounced, "browkers"), or "powwowers." Charmers were not trained physicians and yet they were recognized by their community as people who possessed a God-given gift that enabled them to heal the sick using homemade remedies and medicines for a number of medical conditions.

It was believed that the ability to charm ran in families, although sometimes charmers from outside the family, who had expressed an interest in the tradition, may have been accepted as suitable for training by a *Braucher* (the feminine is, *Braucherin*). Charming practitioners could be either male and female, but the transmission and acquisition of the arcane healing knowledge and its practice (including prayers and rituals) was typically transmitted "contrasexually" — that is, male-to-female or female-to-male. Exceptions to this pattern existed, however; a mother could train a daughter or a father could train a son. Training could take anywhere from a few minutes to a year, although this, too, could vary depending upon the candidate and the relationship between the student and teacher — and on any abilities that might be demonstrated by the student.

THE PRACTICE AND NAMING OF GERMANIC CHARMING

Charming, or *Braucherei*, was a Germanic folk-healing practice that borrowed heavily from a number of sources, involved prayers, biblical passages, and drew heavily upon European folk-beliefs. *Powwowing* is a North American term applied to the practice of charming as found in Germanic-speaking communities in the United States and Canada. It does not appear to have been in use as a distinct practice before the immigration of German-speaking pioneers from continental Europe to Pennsylvania (at least as early as the late 1700s).

The vernacular term *powwowing* is considered by some scholars to be problematic since, according to them, it is being used out of its proper ethnic context, and as such, its usage is sometimes seen as culturally appropriative. On one side of the debate, Professor David Kriebel believes that the term *powwowing* is different from the Indigenous term *powwow*, although he believes that there is most likely a strong historical connection between the two linguistically. In contrast, Indigenous scholar Philip Deloria regards the use of the term *powwowing* (when referencing the Germanic folk-healing practice) as culturally appropriative of North American Indigenous Peoples. Deloria regards its use as an extension of the nineteenth-century practice of exoticizing Indigenous Peoples and their ancient spiritual knowledge as something powerful and mysterious. He says it is like "playing Indian without being Indian," which he argues is disrespectful and culturally derivative. Nonetheless, the term *powwow doctor* is often used when referring to a charmer (or *Braucher*).

Braucherei was not exclusively an occult practice. In fact, it was considered by many of its practitioners as a normal and practical way of offering comfort and care. It provided, they believed, a faith-based hope to the otherwise hopeless sufferers who made up their church-going clientele. Through secret rituals, the charmer made dramatic use of prayers and whispered invocations from familiar Bible verses (particularly from the book of Psalms). It was acknowledged by both clients and charmer/practitioners that God, not the *Braucher*, was the healer. The *Braucher* "tried for a cure" but made no guarantee of healing, ultimately leaving the client's fate to God.

Charmers used verbal charms (previously memorized), medicinal plants, and something known as "sympathetic magic." Sympathetic magic supposedly served to transfer the affliction or disease from the victim to another being, such as an animal (usually a white mouse or a guinea pig), a fruit or vegetable (commonly a potato), an egg, or an inanimate object. Charmers also made use of amulets, talismans, and other magically charged apotropaic objects. As well, charmers wrote "Letters to Heaven" (*Himmelsbriefs*) that contained prayers that people could carry with them for protection. For example, clients were commonly instructed to fold the letter in a certain way and put it into a shoe they were wearing. *Himmelsbriefs* were not always healing devices — although *Brauchers* were usually called upon to provide blessings and remove curses, in some cases they were asked to punish their clients' enemies by laying curses against them.

Though the practice of charming was common, many in the Pennsylvania German community were uneasy with it, and those who practised it were often marginalized. Scholar James Nyce has examined the societal role of folk beliefs within the Pennsylvania German diaspora, focusing, in particular, on magic, systems of power, and identity (of charming practitioners). His research has shown that charmers' relationships to and familiarity with non-traditional, often occult-based, methods of healing were familiar to and accepted by the Pennsylvania Germans, yet were equally controversial at the same time. According to Nyce, charmers were generally marginal, complex figures, poorly understood and often feared by many within and outside the Mennonite religious community. The healing effect of charmers and their practices was recognized within their communities, and yet, the charmers, as people, remained an enigma. The fact that most of them practised alone, whispering their healing incantations, eyes closed, while gesticulating symbolic figures into the air, did little to demystify their art to the simple folk who sought only to be relieved of the burdens of fear and illness.

In Waterloo County, one folk healer stood out from the crowd. Christian Eby was a grandson of Mennonite settler Bishop Benjamin Eby (and a cousin of little Edward Eby, victim of bodysnatcher Dr. Christ). This birthright afforded Eby a position of respect within his community. However, it was really his identity (or social notoriety) as a powerful (and controversial) charmer that enabled Eby to bend traditional rules of social convention regarding his proper role as a husband, father, and proprietary businessman.

It is not known where Christian Eby learned his skills. We do know, however, that his primary practice was in his home community of Berlin (more broadly, Waterloo County) and that he was actively practising in the late nineteenth and early twentieth centuries (at least from 1880 forward). Unusual for a charmer, Christian Eby was able to successfully practise this arcane healing tradition while maintaining his membership in the Mennonite church and his position as a local business owner and family breadwinner, although there are some clues that this balancing act was a tenuous one.

There are extant documents, including a collection of 224 letters from clients (and Eby himself), family photos, and, finally, his son Gordon's diaries. Gordon had an interesting vantage point — he was not only Eby's charming "apprentice" and assistant at times; he was also the person closest to Christian (other than Eby's wife and partner, Catherine) and so had first-hand knowledge of his father's abilities, society's expectations of his power, and the responsibility that weighed upon him to fulfil them.

Christian Eby, his faithful dog, Nellie, and a raccoon, c. 1911.

To say that Christian Eby was a complicated man who had a difficult life is an understatement. He exhibited an overwhelming perfectionism, in both his work and in his personal relationships, but was known to abuse alcohol and to have violent mood swings. Gordon, his son, speaks often of his father taking off (disappearing) on "sprees." It seems that many of Christian's sprees lasted upwards of a week — sometimes more, sometimes less. When he did return home, or when Gordon had to go and fetch him from somewhere, Eby was much the worse for wear, having to spend a day or two sleeping it off to recuperate.

Charming, it is said, is emotionally and physically draining for the practitioner, and it has been documented that a period of rest following a "working cure" was needed. Eby was known to work himself into the ground anyway and to neglect his own health. Is it possible that his way to unwind after charming for his clients was to drink heavily and disappear for a few days? In at least a few of Gordon's diary entries, he mentions that his father was going to work a cure for a particular client, but that he did not always come home right away. On at least one occasion, Gordon was sent to fetch his father back from a drinking binge in Elmira that took place after "working" for a client. Was the drinking a part of Eby's charming ritual "work"? We may never know.

What we do know is that although Christian Eby was a force to contend with, Eby was still just a man.

Christian Eby was born in 1842; as mentioned, he was the grandson of the prominent and highly respected Waterloo County Mennonite pioneer Bishop Benjamin Eby. In fact, Christian was from a long line of men who had served as Mennonite bishops, reverends, or elders in their churches, including some who were somewhat controversial in those roles. His cousin (actually Bishop Benjamin Eby's cousin), Samuel "Indian Sam" Eby, for example, was the pioneer mentioned earlier in this text who served as both a translator and minister to many of the Indigenous people in Waterloo County in the early part of the nineteenth century. He also sold them whisky.

Christian's brother, Ezra, spent many years as a teacher before entering the newspaper business. His was an orderly mind, with a keen interest in the history of his community. Ezra meticulously gathered a vast record of genealogical material and published it in 1895 as the history of many,

Christian Eby as a young man.

if not most, of the Pennsylvania German settlers to this area. Its formal title is *From Pennsylvania to Waterloo: A Biographical History of Waterloo Township*, but it is perhaps better known as "the Eby Book." Christian and Ezra's father, Isaac, followed in his father, Benjamin's, footsteps and was both a minister and a farmer. Christian eventually purchased Isaac's farm once he was married.

Eby married a relatively distant cousin, Catherine Clemens (spellings vary). Their large, extended family consisted of their biological children, Christian's father-in-law, Abraham Clemens, and several of their nephews. Catherine's elderly father came to live with them after her mother, Magdalena Eby, passed away. Several years later, Catherine and Christian opened their home yet again. Catherine's sister, Veronica Stengel, spent much of her adult life in and out of the Hamilton Insane Asylum (where she eventually died), and at some point, Christian and his wife took in several of their nephews to help Veronica out, eventually adopting one of them. Nephew Clayton Stengel sometimes also went by the name of Eby.

There were a lot of mouths to feed at the Eby homestead and, alcoholic sprees aside, Eby never left his family. In fact, he appears to have fulfilled his role, at least nominally, as a provider for his family.

Eby had an affinity for growing things and he built a thriving business as a market gardener. He was rather innovative, being one of the first in this area to use a greenhouse to grow exotic plants and fruits, such as lemons, for sale. His son, Gordon, notes in his diaries that this was a curious risk his father took, but one that paid off well. Christian also sold seeds and, eventually, remedies and medicines that were called for under the auspices of his charming "work."

It could be said that Eby was a "man-of-all-trades," and he was used to customizing his skills to provide for his large (and extended) family. Brother Ezra noted that Christian also "followed the practice as a custom butcher in the winter months," presumably as a means to make money when his gardening business was not as profitable. This would further indicate Eby's ability to take risks through creative means. This creativity was something that he also channelled into his healing gifts. Unlike most traditional charmers, he did not create all of his own remedies. Some were salves he made up from borrowed recipes, or tonics he purchased for resale. His son's diary for August 5, 1912, notes the purchase of Oriental Bitters "which Mother and Dad sell."

As a market gardener and custom butcher, Christian was able to make a modest living to support his large and ever-changing family needs, but, still, there were financial problems (some of which were, no doubt, of his own doing). Christian was not responsible with money and did not always pay his bills on time. Before her death in 1918, two years before his, Catherine clearly noted in her will, addressed to her children and particularly to Gordon, as executor, that Christian was not to have any control over money following her death. During their marriage, Christian had taken out numerous loans, and there had been some court actions for outstanding debts. Many of these had been taken care of and paid for by Catherine on Christian's behalf.

Though he may not have handled money well, Christian, or Chris, as he referred to himself, was a very successful charmer. He had a vast and diverse clientele from all walks of life. Most charmers practised among their immediate family members or in their local community, but Eby's reputation was huge, and word-of-mouth is very powerful. Many of his clients came from outside Waterloo County — from as far as Chicago in the United States, Saskatchewan in western Canada, and, closer to home, such places as Walkerton, Markham, New Hamburg, and so on. He offered treatments for a whole range of conditions: simple complaints such as rashes and stomach aches, and more serious conditions such as arthritis, cancer, dropsy (edema), and nervous problems. It seems that just about everything was fair game.

There was one particular condition, however, for which Eby admitted he had no remedy. Eby and his wife had a special needs daughter, Isabella, who had succumbed to, but survived, the ravages of spinal meningitis. Bella's presence made Eby keenly aware of the limitations of his charming powers. In a letter to Eby, a client mentions that she was told by her father that Eby had told him that there were times when he couldn't heal a particular person as he had "a daughter like that." How poignant a confession is that, for a man with a great reputation as a healer?

Eby's charming business was most often practised in his barn at 409 Mill Street, at the back of his property. That Eby had the freedom (and privilege) to be alone with a client was due, in part, to his Mennonite pedigree as the grandson of a respected bishop, but it can also be argued that, as a male who was known for his take-charge attitude (not to mention a reputation for powerful healing), he was not questioned. Apparently, Eby's clients were comfortable enough to be alone with him: both men and women. There is no evidence that any children were alone with him, but parents (fathers and mothers) sought his services for their suffering children. It is not known how young the children were when he charmed for them, but at least two instances detail situations where he was practising or called to practise on children: Carrie Steinhagen, who was in her late teens, and a "young" boy who lost his foot in a threshing accident.

Eby conducted his practice not only at home but also via mail. This arrangement was unique. His consultations included clients who would sometimes write letters stating that they had received the "medicines" but had forgotten what they needed to do with them. They would write to him, and he would write back with detailed instructions. (The mail system in the early twentieth century was relatively quick. The turnaround time would range from a few days to a week, even outside of town.)

Whether he met with clients personally or corresponded with them via mail, Eby worked tirelessly to help those who sought his help. It is clear, judging by Eby's correspondence with his clients, that he took a strong personal interest in them. Indeed, he offered help for their afflictions that went far beyond what could be expected based on the fees that he charged. As a healer of "last resort," Eby provided his clients considerable comfort.

How did Eby charm?

Brauchers were consulted by those seeking cures for illness and for protection against spells. Eby "charmed" for his clients in a number of unusual ways. His distance healing services are one example. In these cases, clients mailed urine samples and hair cuttings for him to "process" in diagnosing problems and devising treatments. There is no record of how he "processed" these samples or what he actually did with them. It is known, however, that Eby did practise sympathetic magic, and in some of the distance cases he may have employed that.

As mentioned, practitioners of sympathetic magic claim to have the ability to transfer disease to an animal or an inanimate object. It known that Eby used guinea pigs and mice for this purpose. Considered to be an act of conjuring, sympathetic magic is obviously more mysterious than a simple do-it-yourself herbal remedy. Sympathetic magic can more accurately be described as a form of occult healing or, as some have called it, witchcraft.

How does sympathetic magic work? It's quite simple: a white mouse (or some other animal or living thing) is rubbed on the afflicted part of a person's body and then the *Braucher* whispers and repeats words of prayer (incantations). The belief is that the disease then leaves the patient and is transferred into the animal. Eby is known to have done this. One of his patients actually mentions the white mouse in one of his letters to Eby. Eggs and potatoes were also used as recipient vessels. In all cases, the animal or living thing used for the transference was disposed of following the charming session.

It has been said that the power of transferring disease to an object (known as "passing through") could and often did take its toll on the healer's own health, leaving him or her exhausted and sometimes ill. It might be that Christian abused alcohol to self-medicate, seeking relief from the effects of his charming. It may also be that Eby had an undiagnosed medical condition like depression. Certainly he suffered from other conditions — Eby's doctor prescribed for him a change of diet and lifestyle for what sounds like the effects of a chronic ulcer and irritable bowel syndrome. It seems that Eby tried to cure himself of these ailments, but his doctor urged Eby to abandon his attempts to charm himself since, according to the doctor, it was doing him no good. Eby disregarded that advice.

Along with sympathetic magic, Eby used "magical texts" (also called *grimoires*), which are associated with "black magic." His use of these caused even his supporters to be wary of him and his "powers." Two of the most famous grimoires in history are the *Sixth and Seventh Books of Moses* and *Der Lange Verborgene Freund* ("The Long Lost Friend"). Eby is known to have used both.

The first, a two-volume work, is an esoteric text attributed to Moses. It was believed that it was so powerful that it had been kept hidden and not included with the other five that Moses wrote in the Bible. The two books were said to have originated from the Jewish mystical tradition known as Kabbalah,[26] and were believed to have influenced a number of later magical texts as well as some mystical elements of Christianity. Supposedly, the books are full of incantations that enable the summoner to invoke and dismiss spirits. According to legend, Moses gained his magical knowledge when living among the Egyptians. The first five books of the Bible contain general history, laws, the creation, etc. The sixth and seventh books are not considered canonical — as with the Apocrypha — and are said to contain "occult" or hidden knowledge. According to legend, these works were handed down by Moses from father to son until the time of King Solomon, when they were turned over to the priests and, finally, to Talmudic scholars.

Particularly interesting features of these volumes include unique illustrations of "seals" (magical drawings with associated incantations), Hebrew letters, writings from a supposedly lost language — and lists of names of demonic entities. Historically, there is evidence that grimoires were used in early Christianity by the Gnostic sects — the Book of Enoch (attributed to Enoch, great-grandfather of Noah) being particularly important. The magical text *The Sixth and Seventh Books of Moses* is purportedly part of that tradition.

Eby also possessed and used *The Long Lost Friend*, which was published in Pennsylvania (in German) at least as early as 1820. Compiled by German immigrant John George Hohman (or Johann Georg Hohman) from earlier Germanic magical texts that had been popularized sometime in the seventeenth centuries, it is an occult book generally associated with the practice of *Braucherei*. Many Pennsylvania-based *Brauchers* owned and used copies.

But, occult books aside, the most important book of magic used by charmers was the Holy Bible. Although he (or she) would have owned other copies of the Bible, the *Braucher*'s "work" copy would be held separately and would be used only in charming. During a healing session, the *Braucher* would say to his client that he would "try for a cure." Specific Biblical passages would be recited three times, along with other prayers, incantations, and hand gestures. Ultimately, it was considered to be up to God whether the cure would be delivered. In other words, the magic was purported to come from God, not the *Braucher*, who was only a conduit for the divine healing power.

Perhaps the best way to sum up Christian Eby is to say that he was a product of his ability to shape, manipulate, and use the freedoms and privilege afforded to him because of his ancestral pedigree as a man of position in his community. Building upon this, Eby carved out a unique niche for himself, albeit a marginal and divergent one from that of his religious ancestors. Whether Eby was a charlatan (which I personally do not believe) or a gifted healer, the letters to Christian Eby from his clientele show that many believed in his ability to help them. No doubt this is the legacy he would have preferred to leave, as he took his true healing secrets with him to the grave.

Eby certainly was not the only (and arguably not the last) in this region to practise the healing art of charming. Mennonite scholars like Marlene Epp have studied Mennonite midwives in the Waterloo area in the late nineteenth and the early twentieth centuries. Many of these midwives, some of whom were contemporaries of Eby, also practised various forms of charming, offering treatments such as burn remedies or bone setting. One example is Elisabeth Rempel Reimer, who was described as being a "midwife, nurse, and undertaker." (She also had had a fur coat- and hat-making business in Russia prior to coming to Canada.) Among others mentioned in connection with the charming practice are Catherine Wagler Lichty (mentioned only as "Mrs Lichty" in historian W.J. Wintemberg's *Waterloo County Folklore*), Katherine Kesselring, and midwife healer Barbara Bowman Shuh, born in 1857, who inherited the gift of charming, which she used primarily to treat bleeding, burns, and scalds.

These women were often described as those "who made things right," because they were frequently called upon to provide medical treatments that went beyond simple "baby catching," as it was known. They were known as women who could "alleviate suffering," which extended to more traditional medical services, such as pulling teeth, tending to injuries, and offering advice and treatment for various maladies: stomach ailments, headaches, irregularity, nervous disorders, and, yes, even unwanted pregnancy. Bone setting, a precursor of twentieth-century chiropractic techniques, was a common accompaniment to a midwifery practice. Apparently, these women were more collaborative in their practices than many of their male counterparts who practised as charmers. Among known male practitioners were Joshua Rudy, Joseph Brohman, and even a former mayor of Berlin, Jacob Yost Schantz (credited with having an effective folk cure for cancer), to name just a few.

By the beginning of the twentieth century, most Waterloo County Mennonites were already distancing themselves from folk medicine as Eby and others practised it. In my own research, I have found that Christian Eby's polarizing and arguably rogue reputation persists to this day, and it is sometimes difficult to find someone within the Old Order community to speak about the historical practice of powwow or charming — as many today claim that it is associated with Hexerei (witchcraft) and, therefore, with the devil. Many (but not all) have said to me that they do not want to talk about it or will not talk about it at all. This is unfortunate, since, at one time, the practice was more widely accepted among rural Mennonites than the practice of medical physicians, and therefore would have been a common phenomenon.

Things really began to change for Christian Eby after his wife, Catherine, died in 1918. As she was the stable one in the family, it could be argued that following her death, Christian lost his own caregiver and strongest support system. A devout Christian and a devoted wife and mother, she had paid many of Christian's financial debts over the years and kept her family intact behind the scenes, as any woman would have been expected to do in her time (especially a Mennonite woman of faith). After her death, Catherine's will dictated that Christian was "to be taken care of for the rest of his life but was not to have control whatsoever of any money." No doubt this was Catherine's final act to protect Christian from his own self-destructive tendencies. The "powerful, independent" man was effectively assigned a new caretaker from beyond the grave, and it was his own son, Gordon, who was to make sure that his mother's final wishes were carried out.

It seems that whatever diminished physical (and for that matter, emotional) condition Eby was in prior to his wife's death — after years of alcohol abuse, lack of sleep, and neglecting to maintain a proper diet — his health continued to deteriorate following the loss of Catherine. He died only two years after her in 1920.

Perhaps the most revealing letter to Christian Eby is the letter written to him *not* asking for help but *offering* it to him. It was a final prescription for Christian Eby, from his own medical doctor, written and received near the end of his life. It is a most unusual letter and one that I think people today would be hard-pressed to imagine receiving from a family physician. It is hand-written and ten pages long. It details the physician's observation that Eby suffered from a decided lack of "proper self-care" to the extent that he had incurred a number of persistent problems with his liver (which is not surprising considering his rocky relationship with alcohol) and ongoing problems with his digestion (purportedly either from too rich or too poor a diet that lacked common nutrients or fibre). The doctor's letter also describes remedies for chronic constipation and a condition known then as dyspepsia (upper abdomen bloating with acid reflux, or what we might call gastritis). One might wonder what a modern doctor would make of the underlying pathology that may have contributed to Eby's lack of self-care. Was he possibly suffering from an undiagnosed mental health condition such as depression, or had stress become a way of life for him rather than an intermittent problem? It is impossible to know for sure, but his doctor clearly states that Eby needed to stop drinking and avoid the use of his own medicines to relieve his symptoms. His physician believed the medicines were contributing to his declining health. In fact, he went so far as to declare them "useless."

Did Eby listen to his own doctor? The verdict: no. Had he listened to his doctor's advice, he might have bought himself a few more years, but, in so doing, would have negated everything he stood for with respect to charming. Christian Eby was seventy-eight years old at the time of his death on August 25, 1920. It is interesting to note that he sustained a stroke on January 1, 1920, and that he lingered in poor health until his death. The stroke paralyzed his left leg and arm, according to the attending physician H.G. Lackner. Catherine Eby had also died as a result of a stroke, two years earlier in 1918.

Christian Eby, the "powerful healer and charmer," is buried at First Mennonite Cemetery in Kitchener, in the church cemetery his grandfather founded in 1813.

11

CRYSTAL BALLS, SPIRIT GUIDES, AND PSYCHIC HEALERS: THE PRIME MINISTER, THE ARTIST, AND THE NURSE-TURNED-PSYCHIC

> Ask and it will be given to you; seek and you will find; knock and the door will be opened to you.
>
> — Matthew 7:7 (NIV)

> Spirituality leaps where science cannot yet follow, because science must always test and measure, and much of reality and human experience is immeasurable.
>
> — Starhawk

AS WE SAW IN THE PREVIOUS CHAPTER, people have an abiding fascination with the powers of belief, healing, and magic, all of which stem of course from the ultimate mystery of all — death. This fascination was even more prevalent before the modern era and the advanced understanding of disease transmission, epidemiology, and so forth that we now possess.

But at a time when one could not explain how or why things happened — an untimely death, a miraculous cure, or a devastating crop failure — it was natural to question whether God's (or perhaps, the Devil's) power was at work, orchestrating the lives of everyday human beings, indulging in a big cosmic game that only supernatural beings could play, and where humans were little more than pawns.

Belief in the occult theories, even in passing, are common enough (did you check your horoscope today?), and they continue to affect people from all strata of society — from the poorest and least educated to those in positions of power. Supernatural beliefs are not new, nor are they isolated — even today. They have evolved from commonly held mythology that has been handed down from generation to generation, immortalized in the form of folklore, told and retold in cultural forms like stories and morality plays. We know them mostly as fairy tales, and the "most rational" among us take them with a grain of salt (as a grain of salt was once a measure of worth). These tales may scare us and they may entertain us. We may dismiss them. And yet, they persist.

In centuries past, religious beliefs — the promise of heaven for the virtuous, damnation and hell for the sinful — were used by those who feared the loss of religious or sociopolitical control to inspire the persecution of suspected opponents, who were often society's most marginalized. Often, these people were accused of witchcraft and conjuring. Those so identified were often tortured to incite a confession. With that, the powerful (and sometimes the masses) were able to justify the execution of those accused, most of whom were innocent.

There was a duality of spiritual belief: God existed on one side and his enemy, the Devil, on the other. In North America, the Salem Witch Trials of 1692–93 effectively marked the end of witch-hunting trials and their associated executions. As with many cultural practices that had travelled over the Atlantic from Europe, formalized witchcraft hysteria moved into the background realm of "superstition," and people began to look at the supernatural differently.

For the great majority of people who lived before the nineteenth century, magic was an ordinary part of everyday life, and it was very, very, real. In Waterloo County and beyond, folk healers like Christian Eby (particularly in the Victorian era) were common enough and had their place alongside medical doctors, even with regular church-goers.

The realm beyond death was another thing entirely, however. Death was a great unknown — mysterious and sometimes frightening. On the other hand, death was something that everyone was well acquainted with. People died young and there were few cures for those who became ill or suffered serious accidents. This was true for everyone — the rich and the poor. Death did not seem to discriminate, and people were intimately aware of the fragility of life. Indeed, in those days, before the advent of funeral homes, people sometimes spent days with dead bodies — they often laid their beloved dead out on tables in the sitting room or parlour to be viewed and "visited" before interment.

It's no wonder then there were so many stories about the dead. Oh, the ghost stories! The woman in white, wandering aimlessly, grieving for her lost lover; or the grandfather whose pipe smoke could still be detected while (it was believed) he stayed around to watch over his daughter and grandchildren. There were sightings and sounds, particularly at night, when, before the advent of artificial lighting and central heating, shadows were long and dark in the corners of cold rooms. One may recall the scene in Charles Dickens's *A Christmas Carol* in which Marley visits Scrooge after dark, banging and clanging around in a dimly lit room.

Nobody does spooky like the Victorians did! Beneath their civilized facades and high-society manners, the Victorians held a fascination with the spirit world that drove many in search of proof that life continues beyond the veil of death. New philosophies and religious movements emerged — drawing followers who believed that traditional Judeo-Christian beliefs were not able to provide the answers to the existential question that haunted them (pun intended). Some, like Hermetic schools of occult study, formed elite and secret societies that attempted, through the practice of esoteric rituals, to delve into ancient forgotten knowledge, intent on learning secrets to life beyond the veil. Other neo-religious movements, such as spiritualism, emerged. Such movements promoted access to and acceptance of the spirit world that, they taught, existed beyond death — where one's dearly departed could be contacted directly through a variety of means. Some believers sought out messages from crystal balls and psychic mediums; others claimed that the emergent science of photography could be used to capture images of the deceased on film. This was known as spirit photography.

Maines-Pincock séance in session with photographic evidence of ectoplasm.

Oddly, the emergent technology of the period, such as photography, was seen as being well adapted to provide this proof. Science, it seems, was believed to be able to confirm the existence of ghosts. It may seem strange, but it's true.

So, what is spirit photography? The primary goal of spirit photography is to capture images of ghosts and other spiritual entities that are believed to be walking among the living but who cannot normally be seen by the naked eye. The belief is that the camera lens sees images in a pure fashion — i.e., it is able to record these images because it is not impaired by prejudice, fear, or doubt. Photography was used to substantiate "proof" of spirit hauntings or ghostly visitations.

The first known photograph of a "spirit" was actually only a photographic accident, something that reflected the limitations of the early photographic process. (The "ghost" was actually a double exposure — two images appeared to be ghosting each other.)

Such double exposures would be produced countless times, by accident and on purpose, leading many to believe that cameras were able to record otherwise invisible spirits. Of course, charlatans were quick to see the possibilities of this as a way to separate the credulous from their money. And there were many credulous people — some desperate to see their loved ones once again and others simply curious about the other world and the spirits that they believed inhabited it. Those who claimed to be able to photograph spirits were able to persuade potential customers quite easily because, particularly in its early days and especially with the older generations, most people did not understand the technology. They considered it to be almost "magic" and "otherworldly." Keep in mind that many adults in the 1850s would have been born in the late 1700s — they would have remembered a very different world.

During the late nineteenth century, commercialism and its associated advertising really emerged. Among those who advertised their wares and services in hopes of profit were spirit photographers. They advertised their special skills in capturing spirits on film, and some of them gained quite a reputation — eventually drawing a high-profile clientele.

There is a story that Abraham Lincoln's widow, Mary Todd Lincoln, distraught after her husband's assassination, sought the help of mediums and spiritual guides in an attempt to contact him. At one point, she went to Boston to see a famous spirit photographer, William Mumler. She arrived in disguise to sit for her photographic portrait. Returning several days after the sitting, as required, she was amazed (and apparently thrilled) that, just over her shoulder, appearing to stand behind her, was a "ghostly" image of her dead husband.

During this era, many different genres of photographic specialties emerged, many of which captured the deceased on film as a keepsake — or what has been referred to as a *memento mori* (roughly translated as "remember, you must die"). For these, photographs were taken to memorialize the departed dearly beloved. These included dead pets, children, spouses, and grandparents. Some of these photos are particularly grisly because they were taken for bereaved parents with the deceased child surrounded by their living siblings! Closer examination of the photos often reveal blurry spots where the living subjects moved during the photographic session. In these cases, the deceased subject remains clear.

Another type of photograph, popular at this time, simulated the style of *memento mori*, although the figures in the photo were not, in fact, dead. In "Absent Mother" or "Hidden Mother" photography, mothers would wear ghostly veils to cover their faces when holding onto a child — a living and presumably squirming child. This particular form of photography, while in some ways creepy to the modern eye, was an attempt to stage the appearance of a normal portrait of a young child. (Normal, that is, if you think a picture of a cute kid with a veiled, darkened figure sitting behind them, holding them upright is normal rather than the stuff of nightmares.) Long exposure times were typical of the era and would have been difficult enough for an adult to sit still for. A moving child presented challenges, particularly for the photographer, who was expected to photograph the child, not the mother. If the veiled mother was visible at all in the final print, the photographer would have faced strong criticism for not concealing her well enough. The end result, regardless, would have been a bit ghostly, to say the least.

Photographs were not the only kind of *memento mori* created during the Victorian era; specially crafted jewellery was another popular way of memorializing a dead loved one. These pieces included the victim's hair, which may have been braided into a locket or wreath (or even set with some of their teeth among semi-precious stones or pearls). These were intended to be loving tributes and, particularly in the case of the *memento mori* photographs, comforting images that evoked memories of the deceased.

It it is easy to dismiss all of this as crude and distasteful, and yet, even though there were those who set out to deceive and take advantage of a grieving clientele, there were also those who believed in what they did and sought to offer a service that provided some comfort in a difficult time. This paired well with those who searched for ways and means to contact their dead — at almost any cost.

For those seeking such contact, possible ways of doing so included the use of a psychic medium, a séance, or a spirit reading. By the end of the nineteenth century, however, belief in spiritualism and attendance at séances remained but had become more of a form of entertainment: hostesses would invite willing guests to come for a tarot card reading or to attend a séance that promised a ghostly visitation.

Spirit photography was also used in these situations. To begin, mediums entered a trance state, claiming contact. A photograph was taken. The effect? Splashed throughout the photo of séance-attendees would be bright lights, or streaks that looked like they had been left by broad strokes of an invisible paintbrush. These streaks were known as "ecto-plasm," the spirit residue during a spiritual encounter with a ghost.

The term *ectoplasm* was coined in 1894 by the Nobel Prize–winning immunologist Charles Robert Richet, who devoted many years to studying the belief in the paranormal and "photographic proof" of spiritualist phenomena. He theorized that some spiritual mediums gave off or projected a material substance during the process of mediumship that could be captured on film — the ectoplasm seen in photographs taken during an active séance. Ironically, he believed this substance was not a physical but a neurological residue produced by the medium him- or herself. He did not believe that it was caused by spirit activity!

Other researchers and believers disagreed, and declared the substance to be proof of spirit intervention and contact, captured by photography: the lens of the camera could "see" things the naked eye could not. What is most striking is that only some of the ectoplasmic photography can be explained as the product of camera defects or photographic error. There remains some photo "evidence" that lacks a satisfactory explanation of what was actually captured on film or how it definitively occurred.

With the advent of the First World War, interest in spiritualism, mediums, and spirit photography was renewed. Many who had lost loved ones in the war were seeking closure and whatever contact they could get with those they had lost. Many were bereaved sweethearts; others were parents. Not surprisingly, visits to fortune tellers began to dramatically increase as well, since some of the spiritual seekers did not know if their missing loved ones were even dead, and therefore held on to hope that they were still alive.

The seekers came from all walks of life. Many of them helped to shape our modern world of culture, art, literature, and politics. I have already mentioned that Abraham Lincoln and his wife, Mary Todd Lincoln, were believers in spiritualism, but so were authors Sir Arthur Conan Doyle, Charles Dickens, and Mark Twain. For some, such as Conan Doyle, this belief followed from their religious upbringing. Conan Doyle had been raised as a Catholic and had accepted earthly apparitions as a facet of his religious belief — the Virgin Mary and various saints were known to appear to their most devoted followers.

In Waterloo County, a believer of great renown and respect was landscape painter Homer Watson. Watson was a world traveller, painter, and author, perhaps best known for his vivid but ethereal landscapes and pastoral settings. What may or may not be as well known was his private-life attendance at séances and abiding interest in the occult as a gateway to achieve contact with the dead.

Following the death of his beloved wife, Roxanne, Watson turned to the use of Ouija boards and professional mediums in a desperate attempt to contact her and other spirits. At one point, he believed that he had indeed seen her and contacted her: after that, he went on to create some of his best work. He became a very active supporter of spiritualism, holding many séances at his home, where the Homer Watson gallery is today. Following Homer's death in 1936, his sister Phoebe continued to live in the house, and it is believed that her spirit haunts the Homer Watson House and Gallery today. Many are drawn to Homer's artistic and spiritual legacy, but not as many realize that Phoebe was also an accomplished artist in her own right. The home is a popular spot for modern ghost-hunters, having been featured numerous times on film and in the media. Some have claimed outright that they have captured mysterious images on film records of their visits.

Watson was not the only high-profile figure with Waterloo County roots who believed in the supernatural or spiritual contact. A long-time acquaintance of Homer Watson, William Lyon MacKenzie King, was himself no stranger to séances.

As prime minister, King was necessarily a public figure and had to meet and speak with many people, but he was by nature private; indeed, he was often downright reclusive in his private life. This secret world has come to be known via the voluminous diaries that he kept.

A highly educated man, he held multiple university degrees and was the only Canadian prime minister so far to hold an earned doctorate from Harvard (political economy, 1909). Despite his education, King was also a fervid believer in spiritualism and the occult. King, who never married, was very close to his mother and to one of his sisters, who predeceased him, and he tried to contact them many, many times through séances, many of which were facilitated by one of his favourite mediums, Etta Wreidt. He also made numerous attempts to contact his beloved deceased dogs (three Irish terriers, all called Pat) through the use of a crystal ball and Ouija board. King owned several crystal balls, some of which have been on display at his former residence, Laurier House, in Ottawa.

William Lyon McKenzie King.

King and Homer Watson first met when King's father, John, took William, then a young boy (eight years old), to Watson's studio to admire the artist's work. Homer Watson was twenty-seven. John impressed on William what an asset Watson was to both local and national audiences. In later years, as King visited an elderly Watson in 1933, shortly before the latter's death, he remarked how memorable it had been to visit Watson as a boy. King even bought a mystical moonlight canvas as a memento of the evening.

Watson had been an advocate for spiritualism since his first visit to the spiritualist community of Lily Dale in New York State in his youth. When he returned home, he arranged for similar séances to be held at his house. Over the years, King was invited to and attended séances hosted by Watson at the gallery. King became a close confidant to Watson as someone with whom he could discuss his own affinity for spiritualism.

Many fortune tellers advertised their services. Jenny O'Hara Pincock was a locally renowned medium who began her practice in St. Catharines before coming to Kitchener in the late 1920s following the death of her husband Newton in 1928. She was active throughout the 1930s and until her death, about 1948. She was often joined at her séances by her sister, Minnie O'Hara Maines, who was also an experienced psychic medium. Minnie's husband, Fred Maines, had been ordained as a minister while serving overseas for the YMCA during the First World War. Reverend Maines also participated in and facilitated at many local séances, which were often taped and photographed. The Maines-Pincock family exemplified how spiritualist practices had continued to evolve by the 1930s, making use of both video (film) and audio (tape recording) technology to capture purported spirit activity.

Thomas Lacey was a contemporary of the Maines-Pincocks and practised in both Kitchener and Waterloo during this same time period, although he continued to practise well into the 1960s. Lacey rose to prominence as a voice and trance medium. He also chose to record his sessions. Originally from England, Lacey served for a time as a medium in Lily Dale.

One of Lacey's claims to fame was his use of cone-shaped séance trumpets. Mediums sometimes used these in their sessions, claiming that they enabled them to "listen" to the voices of the dead (they operated rather like microphones for the deceased). It was said that these séance trumpets had the ability to transcend the boundaries between the physical and metaphysical realms. The tips of séance trumpets were often painted in vibrant colours (sometimes using radioactive radium, so they glowed in the dark like those early alarm clocks). Supposedly, upon the arrival of the spirits, the trumpets would spin around and move about the room, emanating voices and whispered messages from the dead. Lacey claimed that his spirit guide was actually his deceased brother, Walter, who had departed at a very young age. The Maines-Pincocks used séance trumpets in some of their sittings as well.

Another noted local medium was the former mayor of Berlin-Kitchener and self-proclaimed cancer specialist, Dr. John Emil Hett, who owned a house at 223 King Street East in Kitchener. He wrote prolifically about his treatments for cancer but never specifically revealed the ingredients that were in his "cure." Eventually, he reluctantly allowed it to be analyzed. It turned out to be medically harmless, but its efficacy, if any, was never proven. Dr. Hett rented space in his house to the Mennonite Central Committee, which was located on the main floor. He kept a separate entrance that led into his office, and on the second floor of the same house was another room that was reserved for séances. The cancer doctor was also a confirmed spiritualist.

I personally remember stories about another spiritual psychic. Throughout the 1970s, it was said that people would line up before dawn on the rural road outside a home in Millbank, waiting to see Vera McNichol. She never booked appointments, nor did she time the meetings she had with her clients. She saw one after the other, often into the night. Her husband ushered them in one by one and kept watch over her (and them). Clients reported that she spent time with them, never in a hurry, and gently addressed whatever their problem was. Sometimes, it was a lost object. Other times, it was a missing person.

Vera Ernst was born in Berlin, in 1910. She married John McNichol and later trained to be a nurse and a midwife. At some point, her psychic abilities began to draw clients seeking guidance and spiritual healing from a variety of concerns to her home. Vera was compelled to help them. The only money she earned at this time was through the sales of various books of poetry, history, and biblical stories that she had written over the years (her husband would sell them to clients as they waited to see Vera).

Her psychic abilities were renowned. She was known to deliver messages from beyond the grave, including some from victims of murder. Police officers from all over North America sought her services when they faced difficult situations involving an unsolved murder or missing-person cases with little tangible evidence or leads. She helped the police solve dozens of cases and was so sought-after that she was even listed in card catalogues as a psychic consultant at a number of local libraries as far away as London, Ontario.

Vera may have been a nurse by training, but it was her ability to help people heal through her gift as a medium for which she is most often remembered.

Now we turn to an unusual and controversial artifact of mysterious origin. Its owner, Anna Mitchell-Hedges, claimed that the crystal skull she discovered as a young girl while on an archaeological dig with her adoptive father in Belize was of ancient origin, supposedly over 3,600 years old (though how she determined this is a mystery). When she found the skull in the early 1900s, she claimed that it possessed magical powers and that it may have been made with alien technology on another planet and brought to Earth. She and her father lost track of the skull, but it was later purchased by a colleague of Anna's father at an antiquities auction in 1943. The family friend eventually turned the skull over to Anna, who continued to publicly display it (and tour with it) for much of her life.

In later years, Anna claimed that the skull had the ability to radiate some kind of healing energy, but that the energy was alien (which fit in somewhat with her earlier origin story). Her claims were large. She even claimed to have received guidance from Mayans who stated the skull was that of an ancient high priest of Atlantis and that its power could be harnessed to "will death." Her proof for all of these claims was limited, at best.

The skull was analyzed by British scientists, who decided it had been created with relatively modern technology — right here on Earth. It was also tested at Yale University, where one scholar claimed that it was an exquisite example of early Aztec design, although he admitted that there was no way he knew of to decipher whether it was modern or ancient. The tool marks on the artifact were ambiguous at best, he said, offering few clues.

I, myself, saw the skull when Anna took it on one last local tour. This time, it was displayed at the Frederick Street Mall. (This was just before Anna moved from her Pioneer Park home in Doon and returned to England, taking the skull with her.) I cannot say that I remember anything mysterious or exciting happening (except that the mall was absolutely packed with people shoving each other, trying to get a closer look). What I can say was that, from an artistic perspective, it really was beautiful — if only because it sat prominently displayed in a plexiglass case, on a black velvet cloth that covered the plinth below it. I remember a light shining overhead, but that may have just been the reflection from the overhead lights of the shopping mall. Regardless, the lights did highlight the skull's exquisite design.

Perhaps the skull's notoriety lay in its mystery. It was the inspiration for the Indiana Jones movie *Indiana Jones and the Crystal Skull.* In fact, Hollywood was fascinated with it, and a lot of famous people spent time alone with the skull (with Anna's permission), including actors William Shatner, Peter O'Toole, and Shirley MacLaine.

There are a few dozen other such skulls in private collections worldwide, whose composition varies from clear, like the Mitchell-Hedges skull, to smoky. Some are cruder in design and execution than others. As an art motif, skulls figure prominently throughout various forms of Mesoamerican, particularly Mexican, artwork and cultural iconography, as symbols of regeneration. Various mythologies reference mysterious powers said to be dormant in skulls. Some hold that the skulls have the power to foretell the future. Some legends foretell a time when multiple skulls will converge to emit powerful forces for healing, heralding the return of ancient ancestors who will rule over the Earth in peace, awakening it for a new era.

PART 5

History as Storytelling

12

THE LEGEND OF OROMOCTO SPRING

> We are all storytellers. We all live in a network of stories. There isn't a stronger connection between people than storytelling.
>
> — Jimmy Neil Smith

> Once upon a time there was what there was, and if nothing had happened there would be nothing to tell.
>
> — Charles De Lint

IT IS SOMETIMES THROUGH the telling of stories that we encounter our earliest memories of family and community. Of course, memories are not always accurate. Memory is fluid, and the images from the past can be fleeting. It is little wonder, then, that stories based on memories are not always accurate, either; but, accurate or not, they are no less present.

Stories are the currency we use to trade our communal knowledge of community: its geography, its people, and, yes, its development over time. Stories help us to access feelings, memories, and, perhaps in some ways, the lives of those who went before us. Such stories may provide comfort, entertainment, enlightenment, and they may also help us to confront the most uncomfortable aspects of human behaviour and ideas. Sometimes, stories are used as propaganda and marketing tools.

In this book I have detailed some of the stories of Waterloo people who lived on the margins of society. I think it is equally appropriate to make mention of the footprint that the people of Waterloo have left on the natural habitat of the area. Increasingly, with the escalation in development, the natural world has also come to be considered of marginal importance. But there are those who remember a less-developed region. These people, and those they have shared those memories with, have invoked the power of those memories to make a case for heritage conservation.

One case stands out. Cressman's Woods was located near the rural homestead of landscape artist Homer Watson. In 1913 a concerned citizen group (the Waterloo County Grand River Park Company) saved the woodland from a proposed development scheme. The land was about to be sold at public auction, and it appeared was most likely to be purchased by a local sawmill owner, who would have no doubt made a handsome profit harvesting its old-growth forest.

Among the members of the citizen group were industrialist A.R. Kaufman (of Kaufman Rubber fame), D.B. Detweiler (an early supporter of Ontario Hydro), and, of course, Homer Watson, who lived nearby. It's likely that Watson would have had a personal attachment to this land, and obviously the others in the group did, too, but they realized that to save the woods they needed public support. At the time, Waterloo County was still relatively surrounded by old-growth forest, so the group realized that they needed to find some way to make this particular area stand out as unique and deserving of conservation. What did they come up with? A good story.

LOCAL FOLKLORE: "THE LEGEND OF OROMOCTO SPRING"

The group began advertising the story of an "Indian" legend about the origin of the Oromocto Spring. The spring still exists, running through an area that has had its name changed many times over the years — originally it was Attiwandron Park, then Cressman's Woods. Today, we know it as Homer Watson Park. Homer Watson Park is in Doon, once its own settlement but now a subdivision in the southeastern area of Kitchener. It is along the banks of the Grand River, near the Waterloo Region Museum and Doon Heritage Village.

The story was created not to cast a spotlight on some bit of forgotten local Indigenous history, but to create a tragically romantic tale for marketing. In 1937 the legend was resurrected for one of the Waterloo Historical Society's annual volumes by Walter Cunningham, who told the story to a new audience.

Cunningham began his tale:

> In the misty past, the Iroquois Indians hunted game in this region. There was a band that was notorious for their prowess in the chase, their Woodcraft, cunning, and cruelty to prisoners. The Upper Canada tribes were less bloodthirsty and feared the Iroquois. When a warning of their approach was received, runners were dispatched to other friendly camps summoning their warriors to assist them in repelling the dreaded marauders.

Cunningham goes on to relate that a young Attiwandaron girl, named Nashwaaksis, was chosen to warn another tribe (the Petuns) about the impending approach of their enemies, the warring Iroquois. In order to warn them, she had to travel on foot from the Doon area to a settlement site near Elmira where the Petuns had already set up a seasonal camp.

It so happened that Nashwaaksis was in love with a Petun warrior by the name of Oromocto, who, because he was a member of the Petuns, was in great danger from the Iroquois. As Nashwaaksis and Oromocto were from different tribes, they were not really able to meet openly with each other, so their love affair was a secret. Because she was going to warn the Petuns, she was able to meet with her lover — in person — on the pretence that she was on a reconnaissance mission from her tribe (which, it so happened, she was). Her journey took her several days, so when she finally arrived at the Petuns camp, she stayed to rest for a time. Oromocto presented her with a gift of beautiful handmade moccasins to replace the ones she had worn out during her journey. On the eleventh day, she and Oromocto left the Petun village to return to her home at the Attiwandaron camp. There they intended to marry once the Iroquois were defeated.

On the first night of their journey, they laid camp and stayed in the Cressman's Woods, with Nashwaaksis sleeping and Oromocto standing guard over her. Once she fell into a deep slumber, Oromocto decided to patrol the area for security. Much to his misfortune, he stumbled upon the encroaching Iroquois in the dark. Oromocto managed to return long enough to carry the barely awake Nashwaaksis to safety in the woods before engaging in battle with his enemies. He fought valiantly but was slain in battle. Nashwaaksis mourned for her fallen lover and was so grief-stricken, Cunningham told his audience, that she let out a "heart-broken scream" before she fell prostrate and dead over the body of her beloved Oromocto.

Two days later, Attiwandaron tribe members who were searching for them came upon their lifeless, entwined bodies. They lifted both bodies into the air to honour them for their valiant deaths, and as they did so, a spring burst forth from the earth — at the very same spot where they had died. To the Attiwandaron, the spring was a powerful sign and they proclaimed it to be "as clear as the character of beautiful Nashwaaksis, as pure as the love of the twain, and cold as the heart of the Iroquois." From thence forward, the water was believed to have "ingredients that restored health" and could ensure "happiness." They named the waters after the brave warrior: Oromocto Spring.

Since then, according to the story, many visitors to the area have said that when you walk in the area of the spring you can still hear Nashwaaksis crying for her lost love, Oromocto. There have been claims of sightings of a young Indigenous woman, crying as she walks along the banks of the Grand River as if she is searching for someone. Other accounts state that she is heard in the soft breezes of the blowing wind — when one barely catches the sound of a soft, mournful sob. And then there are those, it is said, who have heard her cries of grief in the water itself as it babbles over stones and rocks.

A compelling tale to be sure. Magical waters, and the untimely, tragic death of two valiant lovers.

But, as previously stated, it was a total fabrication. The "legend" first appeared locally, in print, in a 1917 newspaper article designed to promote tourism to the "new" park and boost the financial coffers of the local First World War effort. The area is beautifully pastoral, in and of itself, and the creation of such a tragic tale does nothing really to enhance the natural beauty of the place, which should be embraced and appreciated as is. Unfortunately, the promoters of the park felt that the area "needed a little push" to elicit a strong emotional response from the general public, and so they decided to make one up.

It should be noted that the names and details of the legend are not documented anywhere or in any way within Indigenous folklore, locally or otherwise; but the story, regardless of its origin or intent, lives on — as does, more importantly, the protected park and its spring.

EPILOGUE

AS WE REFLECT UPON THE STORIES IN THIS BOOK, we see that, however disparate they may seem, they all involve people, places, and events that were (and still are) off the mainstream. For those most vulnerable, history can be made to reveal not only the bare details of their stories, but also the ways in which society did (or did not) step in to change the course of their fates. This can be a more personal journey when the subjects are close to home—where names and places are more familiar and possibly harder to escape emotionally.

When trying to understand local history, then, it is often advisable to take a step back from written records and remaining buildings. These are important, but they must be examined in context. I say this, in part, because there are times when all we have left (when we look at history) is stories like those I have shared with you in this book. Buildings and landmarks change, are torn down, or become modified. In rare instances they are even moved to make way for a new highway or light rail transit system or some other infrastructure. And not only do individual buildings change and disappear, the landscape of whole areas can be altered. In these cases, it gets harder to "see" where the stories happened.

The iconic Pioneers' Memorial Tower or "Pioneer Tower." Built in 1926 as a commemorative nod to the early Pennsylvania German pioneers in the area, the tower's construction overlooks the Grand River, which is reminiscent of the route that would have been taken by the pioneers who journeyed here from Pennsylvania during the early part of the nineteenth century.

I mentioned at the beginning of the book that some of the stories in this text are not my stories (meaning that they are not the stories of my ancestors), but I believe that it is important to share the stories that may otherwise be forgotten — further, I believe we need to "hear" the stories that we may no longer be able to "see" because of the changing landscape. In other words, a community and its history are more than its geography or skyline.

It is people who cultivate and build communities, and whether or not the communities grow or die, they exist (and may have existed) because of people. When we hear the stories that we can no longer see, we remember the people who lived them. Real people, real lives, real stories — particularly those you didn't know. This is life on the margins in *Waterloo You Never Knew.*

TIMELINE

1800	The first Pennsylvania German settlers arrive in the area and begin to establish farms on land previously occupied by First Nations Peoples.
1806	Abraham Erb, founder of Waterloo (city), arrives in the Waterloo area from Pennsylvania.
1807	Joseph Schneider and Benjamin Eby arrive in the Berlin area from Pennsylvania.
1816	"The Year Without a Summer," when every month of the year, including the spring and summer, was visited by devastating frosts that killed off tender food-producing crops.
1816	Abraham Erb establishes the first grist mill in Waterloo.
1816	Joseph Schneider Haus (today a Museum and National Historical Site) is built and a sawmill is established.
1820	Abraham Erb's log school is built. This is the first school in Waterloo.
1830	Abraham Erb dies.

1830	Jacob C. Snider buys the mill and land from Erb's estate. This land comprises much of what we know today as Uptown Waterloo.
1830s	Levi Carroll, ex-slave, arrives in the Waterloo County area.
1832	Paola Brown establishes a black settlement in the Crook's Tract (the Winterbourne area of Woolwich Township).
1834	A travelling menagerie arrives in the Galt area and an infected showman brings a deadly disease to unsuspecting citizens. Cholera ravages the community of Galt, leaving two hundred dead.
1835	J.C. Snider starts a distillery to process surplus grain.
1840	John Frederick Augustus Sykes Fayette, graduate of Case Western Reserve University, opens a private school in Berlin called the Wellington Institute. Fayette was educated and a free man at a time when many blacks were just beginning to flee slavery.
1842	Erb's log schoolhouse is moved to Abraham Weber's land and becomes a dwelling. Levi Carroll, an employee of Weber, rents it for five dollars a month.
1842	Christian Eby, the healer and charmer, grandson of Bishop Benjamin Eby, is born.
1843	Joseph Schneider, the pioneer, dies. His son Joseph E. Schneider takes over the family farm and his father's sawmill.
1847	Abraham C. Weber, the youngest child of Abraham Weber, the pioneer, receives the title for his father's land (481 acres), most of which was in Greenbush/Berlin, where the 1820 log schoolhouse was located).
1848	Over 1,500 black residents are recorded as being resident in the Queen's Bush.
1851	Only 237 black citizens recorded as still living in the Queen's Bush area.

1852 Robert Sutherland, first black graduate of Queen's University, is called to the bar in 1855 and comes to Berlin to set up practice as a lawyer. Many of his clients were blacks from the Queen's Bush area.

1853 With the Grand Trunk Railway's arrival imminent in 1856 (today the Canadian National Railway line that runs parallel to Victoria Street, Kitchener), Abraham C. Weber sells all but six acres of his land to Sheriff George John Grange of Guelph. Weber moves out to the Freeport area (near the Chicopee area in Kitchener today). Apparently, Weber decided to sell because he was not happy that the train was slated to run the length of his property.

1853 Jacob C. Snider sells the land (320 acres in total) and mill that he had purchased from Abraham Erb's estate to his son. His son, Elias Snider, apparently did not like the notion of the distillery.

1853 Elias sells most of the land that he purchased from his father to John Hoffman.

1853 Waterloo County Gaol, also known as Berlin Gaol, opens.

1855 John Hoffman has the land surveyed by M.C. Schofield. This becomes known as "the Hoffman Survey of Waterloo."

1855 Painter Homer Watson is born.

1856 The train and railway transportation come to Berlin. A real boon for business that helps to cement the success of the manufacturing sector of Berlin from the mid-1850s well into the 1960s.

1859 Bodysnatcher Dr. Friedrich Christ goes to the Berlin Gaol for his crimes.

1868 The town of Berlin buys two acres of land from John Hoffman for a municipal cemetery, but it is not used for this purpose. In 1874 the land is used to build the Berlin High School, which we know today as Kitchener Collegiate Institute (KCI).

1869	The Waterloo County House of Industry and Refuge (also commonly referred to as The Berlin House of Industry and Refuge) opens.
1872–73	John Hoffman serves as mayor of Berlin.
1874	Construction begins for the future KCI on King Street West. The building cost $5,804 but does not open until 1876.
1874	William Lyon MacKenzie King, future prime minister of Canada, is born in Berlin. Canada's longest-serving prime minister, he was PM from 1921 to June 1926, September 1926 to 1930, and 1935 to 1948.
1878	Hoffman dies and Joseph Emm Seagram purchases land, including what he will eventually donate for the first hospital in Berlin.
1883	Artist Homer Watson purchases the former Robert Ferrie Jr. House in Doon (along with the two and two-thirds acres upon which it was situated). Robert's father, Robert Ferrie Sr., was a wealthy industrialist from Scotland who founded the community of Doon. Today the house is known as the Homer Watson House and Gallery.
1890	Levi Carroll's third wife, Margaret, dies.
1890	Jacob Eby's farm is purchased by the Waterloo Park Board.
1891	Levi Carroll enters the Waterloo County House of Industry and Refuge along with his stepdaughter, Emiline, and her son, William Aylestock. The log schoolhouse is now vacant and stays that way for the next three years.
1893	Westside (Waterloo) Park opens to the public.
1894	The 1820 log schoolhouse is purchased by the Park Board and moved to Waterloo Park, where it still stands.
1894	Seagram donates some of the land (see previous entry) around where the former log schoolhouse stood to be used for a new hospital. This was the first hospital in the Kitchener-Waterloo area and known then as the Berlin Hospital. Today it is Grand River Hospital.
1897	Levi Carroll dies in the House of Industry and Refuge.

1910	Psychic healer Vera Ernst McNichol is born in Kitchener.
1914–18	First World War
1916	Berlin's name change becomes official and it is now known as Kitchener.
1916	The *Ontario Temperance Act*, which led to the prohibition of the sale of alcohol in Ontario, is passed.
1919	Joseph Seagram dies and his sons take over the distilling business.
1920	Charmer Christian Eby dies eight months after suffering a stroke on New Year's Eve.
1924	The year Anna Mitchell-Hedges claims to have discovered the famed crystal skull at age sixteen while on an archaeological dig with her adoptive father, Frederick Albert Mitchell-Hedges, in Belize.
1927	The *Liquor Control Act* is passed, overturning Prohibition mandated by the *Ontario Temperance Act*. The sale of liquor is restricted to government-run stores. Public drinking remains illegal for seven more years.
1930s	Psychic medium Jenny Pincock performs numerous séances in the Kitchener-Waterloo area. She is joined in her work by her sister, Minnie Maines. Spiritualist Thomas Lacey also performs during this time period.
1970s–1995 (her death)	Nurse, midwife, and psychic healer Vera Ernst McNichol, living in Millbank in neighbouring Perth County, helps clients find lost people and possessions and becomes famous for her high-profile assistance to police in solving murders

ACKNOWLEDGEMENTS

IT WAS A LONG JOURNEY to see this project realized, and I had a lot of help along the way. This help came in timely bits and took many different but equally important forms. Sometimes it took the form of help with editing an awkward passage of text; at other points, it came as words of encouragement and support, extended when I needed them most. Other times, help was extended in the simplest but most basic of supportive gestures in the midst of turmoil. Indeed, there were times when the realities of daily life threatened to slow me down, but with help, I made it through.

To Stephanie Kirkwood Walker, my deepest thanks. I had no idea that day over breakfast that we would hatch such a plan. For your insight, heartfelt recommendations, and gift of storytelling, I thank you.

As the ball began to roll, a whole new world opened up for me. I extend my sincere thanks to the excellent team at Dundurn. Although Margaret Bryant is now hanging her hat at Orca Books, her early guidance was most crucial in helping me navigate unfamiliar territory in the publishing world. Perhaps the Most Patient Man of the Year Award should go to Dominic Farrell, my indomitable developmental editor for the book.

Dominic and I shared many an email and more than a few emotional phone calls when life literally got in the way of the creative process. Always respectful, patient but firm, Dominic helped me leap over a few fires in order to bring the text to completion. For this I extend my deepest thanks. You were truly a guidepost for me when I needed it. Thanks also to Elena Radic, my project editor, who kept me on a short tether and the tight deadlines I needed to deliver a finished product. Along the way, I met a few new Dundurn faces and said goodbye to others, but all have been very supportive and have provided meaningful feedback on all aspects of the book's construction.

To my friends and colleagues who lent me books, offered advice, or shared important research snippets and photos with me, I say a humble thanks. In this, Darryl Bonk has been exemplary. Darryl, you have helped me sort through some research quandaries and locate otherwise elusive photographs. Words cannot completely convey the depth of gratitude I owe to you for doing this for me.

To Marion Roes, I thank you for your continued friendship, support, and research snippets, which have always been welcome and appreciated. I also extend my thanks to rych mills, who often delivered books to me that were invaluable to my understanding of our local history.

With that in mind, no historian, researcher, or author can work without the abiding assistance of the community's archives and libraries. Waterloo region is certainly well represented in this and I have continued to be blessed by the magic wrought by Karen Ball-Pyatt, who has always been generous, particularly with her time, and who has the uncanny ability to anticipate exactly which file or photo I need when I have been in attendance at the Grace Schmidt Room in the Kitchener Public Library on research days.

Maintaining a good working relationship with archivists and librarians makes a researcher's job easier. For this I also thank Charlotte Woodley at the Waterloo Region Archives, Stacey McLennan and Amber Nowak at the Ken Seiling Waterloo Region Museum Collections, Laureen Harder-Gissing at the Conrad Grebel Mennonite Archives, Nick Richbell from the University of Waterloo Special Collections, Dan Schmalz at the Cambridge Archives, and finally, Jennifer Georgiou from the Wellington County Museum and

Archives. For ongoing support and access to the Seagram Collection and other City of Waterloo history, Karen VandenBrink of the City of Waterloo Museum deserves special recognition and my sincere thanks.

To Yoke Kennedy, who helped me through some challenging days (particularly for keeping me sane between deadline demands), I extend my deepest heartfelt gratitude. I also wish to thank the folks at Martin's Garage for keeping me mobile during my research trips around the region. I especially want to thank Paul Martin for some good Mennonite history conversations, particularly those that involved folk medicine of days gone by.

To my friends and colleagues from each of the Waterloo region museums — Schneider Haus, Ken Seiling, Waterloo Region Museum, and MacDougall Cottage — I thank you for your ongoing support, friendship, and never-ending curiosity about our local history. We are a passionate lot, indeed.

I particularly wish to thank the Friends of Joseph Schneider Haus and the Waterloo Regional Heritage Foundation for their financial support on earlier research projects, some of which opened the door for this book. Local history continues to wrap around itself, and each time one trail is followed, another diverges from it. I also note the contributions of Susan Burke — her diligence, perseverance, and keen eye in the preservation and conservation of Waterloo Region Pennsylvania German Folkways and its history. That I personally benefited from her skill and knowledge is something for which I owe her deep gratitude, as it reawakened in me a desire to know more about my own family history as a descendant of Pennsylvania German settlers who came here in 1802 (many of whom never really left).

Above all, I thank my family. You make everything worthwhile. I've worked hard to instill a love and passion for history in you. You are my raison d'être, and there were many times when I felt buoyed by your love and assistance, which enabled me to have the time to work. Thank you, then, to Jenn, her partner Christopher Yetman, Cy, and Carena.

NOTES

1. In the "poorhouse" (another name for the House of Industry and Refuge), children were kept separate from adult men and women.
2. Usually via Windsor, Ontario, to Detroit, Michigan.
3. Louis Aubrey Wood, *The War Chief of the Six Nations: A Chronicle of Joseph Brant* (Toronto: Glasgow, Brook and Company, 1914). For further information also see: King George III of England, *Royal Proclamation of 1763,* collectionscanada.gc.ca/publications/002/015002-2010-e.html.
4. Ibid.
5. Deborah Doxtator, "What Happened to the Iroquois Clans? A Study of Clans in Three Nineteenth Century Rotinonhsyonni Communities," (Ph.D. Thesis, University of Western Ontario, 1996).
6. F. Douglas Reville, *History of the County of Brant* (Brantford: Hurley Printing Company, 1920).
7. The Iroquois, or Haudenosaunee ("People of the Longhouse") were known during the colonial years to the French as the

Iroquois League, and later as the Iroquois Confederacy, and to the English as the Five Nations. This group was originally comprised of the Mohawk, Onondaga, Oneida, Cayuga, and the Seneca. After 1722, they accepted the Tuscarora into their confederacy and became known as the Six Nations.

8. Also known by his Indigenous name *Thayendanegea*, which, in the Mohawk language, roughly translates into "two wagers (sticks) bound together for strength," or possibly "he who places two bets."
9. The British Crown paid out a significant amount of land and cash grants to a number of loyalists following the Revolutionary War as a reward for loyalty and service to the Crown. See: Reville, *History of the County of Brant*.
10. Also known as the Haldimand Tract, it was comprised of six blocks of land that were 674,910 acres in total, extending from the Grand River's mouth at Port Maitland, Ontario, on Lake Erie to the river's source (near the modern-day village of Dundalk, Ontario).
11. Wood, *War Chief of the Six Nations*.
12. There were six blocks in total.
13. Historian Elizabeth Bloomfield, in her book *Waterloo Through Two Centuries,* says that in November 1796, Joseph Brant sold Block 2 to Richard Beasley and his partners James Wilson and Jean-Baptiste Rousseaux — all of whom were merchants at the head of Lake Ontario (near Burlington, Ontario). Beasley, often maligned in local history accounts, did not make an initial down payment for the mortgage on the land but, after hiring Richard Cockerell to survey his holdings, proceeded to sell some of the land (nearly 14,200 acres) to the first group of Pennsylvania German settlers in 1800 (after he had first given some land to his creditors, merchants J. Horning and James Wilson). No doubt he thought that he could come up with the rest of the money he needed from this initial sale. Unfortunately, without clear title to sell he was not authorized to hand over any deeds. Consequently, in 1803, those who had already settled here found themselves squatting on what they had thought was their own land. The settlers confronted Beasley, who then offered the Pennsylvania German settlers, most of whom were

Mennonite, a deal whereby they could purchase the remaining lots, some 60,000 acres, which money he would then use to discharge the whole mortgage and they would own all of Block 2, including those lots from the earlier surveys. After a trip back home and several failed meetings, the Mennonites formed a consortium of twenty-six individuals, most of whom were related, which became known as the German Company. The required ten thousand dollars was raised and Block 2 became theirs. The 60,000 acres were subdivided into 128 farms of equal size and investors in the German Company drew lots for possession. Many chose to immigrate to Canada from Pennsylvania but others sold their interest and chose to stay put.

14. The Missisauga are a sub-tribe of the Anishinaabe.
15. In point of fact, the first families to register title to their land in 1800 were the Bechtel and Biehn familes, followed a few weeks later by the Schörgs and Betzners (Bloomfield, 1995, 34).
16. A wonderful account of the journey made by these hardy and intrepid folk is presented by Ezra E. Eby (a descendant of Bishop Benjamin Eby), who wrote *From Pennsylvania to Waterloo: A Biographical History of Waterloo Township,* published in 1895. Although mistakes in this work exist with respect to some names and dates, it is still a must read for local history. This is accessible online: http://ebybook.region.waterloo.on.ca.
17. The Mennonites had a strong extended community that they knew as "Freundschaft." At first glance, its loose translation is "friendship," but in its use, *Freundschaft* meant something much deeper to the Mennonites. It denoted a sense of community as extended family, to which they were fiercely devoted. For example, if one family needed a barn for their animals, the community would collectively show up and, by providing the labour, build it for them. Reciprocally, you would also provide the same service for them when it was your turn to do so. These types of organized labour forces were commonly known as "bees." In this way, the Mennonites shared more than a common language (a German dialect known as "*Plattdeutsch*") and belief system — they also shared core values and mores with their inner community. The notion of *Freundschaft*

did not, however, include outsiders or strangers per se. Although they dealt with outsiders fairly and honestly (most commonly in business transactions), they were for the most part a "closed" society — they looked out for each other as members of their own extended family-community. Elizabeth Bloomfield does provide some insight into exceptions to this rule whereby orphaned children of non-Mennonite families were adopted into Mennonite families following the death of their parents and some siblings during an outbreak of cholera in 1832. "Building Community on the Frontier," *Ontario Mennonite History* 15, no. 2 (1997): 38.

18. Joseph Schneider, brother-in-law to Bishop Benjamin Eby, settled on Lot 17 GCT (German Company Tract). This includes the land on which Victoria Park is located.
19. Controversial character "Indian Sam" Eby, brother of Bishop Benjamin Eby, settled on Lots 1 and 18 of the GCT. He was colloquially referred to as "Indian" Sam because of his close relationship to the Indigenous Peoples in the area of Waterloo Township. As a distiller of whisky, he sold alcohol to the Indigenous, but his relationship with them was more complex in that it seems that he was also their friend — as Ezra Eby calls him "the Indians' minister, interpreter and lawgiver (Uttley, 1975 [1937]: 22). "He established a distillery in 1804 at a crossroads where he traded whisky in exchange for the Mississaugas' furs. Fellow settlers in 1808 then complained to the provincial legislature that Eby's actions had caused the Mississauga "to get drunk and lie about and not follow their hunting, and [to leave] their young ones starving and begging for food." Many of the local Mississauga converted to Methodism and gave up the use of liquor. They (the Mississauga) also strove to become exemplary models of middle-class culture, leading one German immigrant to Waterloo in 1833 to remark that the Indigenous he had met were "the most peaceable people, a large number of them Christians." (Reginald E. Good, *University of Waterloo Gazette*, October 25, 1995).
20. In 1805 John Erb arrived from Pennsylvania and settled in the Preston-Cambridge area. Credited as the founding father of

Preston, Erb established a profitable grist mill in 1807 that pre-dated the first store and schoolhouse in the area. As of 2009, his grist mill was still in operation (the Dover Flour Mills) and was the oldest mill in operation in the Waterloo Region (Karl Kessler, 2010, *Mennonites and Milling in Waterloo Region*).

21. There is a common misconception that a circus is the same thing as a travelling menagerie. *Travelling menagerie*, in this context, refers to a collection of captive and most often "exotic" animals such as tigers, lions, elephants, etc., sometimes referred to as a "museum of living animals," that would travel on a circuit to various venues where the animals performed acts for the public as exhibits and mainliners of the show. What is distinct between a travelling menagerie and a circus is that while a circus often contains a menagerie and "showmen" (those who handle the animals, their training, and performances), a circus provides additional acts such as clowns, acrobatic acts, and unusual performances like knife throwers, etc. Historically speaking, then, the menagerie and the circus were distinct. In the early years (late eighteenth to early nineteenth centuries), travelling menageries would often set up in barns, stables, or tavern yards, which were not considered appropriate places for women or children to attend. So, eventually, tents were adopted for use to house both the animals and general audience in order to increase attendance (see Stewart Thayer, *Annals of the American Circus, 1793–1860* (Seattle: Dauven & Thayer, 2000).
22. For a more complete account, see: http://generations.regionofwaterloo.ca. (If you select "People who died in epidemics," you will find more than 216 names. Not all of the individuals listed perished in the 1834 Galt epidemic, but many of them did.)
23. Today, with improvements in sanitation, treatment, and early diagnosis, the incidence of cholera has diminished significantly. In Canada, the disease has been all but eradicated. Globally, however, about a hundred thousand people still die each year from this invisible but deadly foe.
24. Midwife or, in this case, obstetrician.
25. Early medical doctors, particularly those in nineteenth-century

Ontario, did not always make enough money to live on and sometimes faced strong competition from their medical peers (or non-qualified quacks and hucksters, as the medical field was full of them). Many turned to unconventional and sometimes illegal means to find ways to make a living. Some moonlighted in other fields of practice, such as dentistry (although it was often barbers who performed those duties since they already had their clients comfortably seated in reclining chairs). Why did they do this? Simply stated: those who extracted teeth could offer them up for sale. Who would buy them? Someone in the denture-making business or someone with money who needed to have dentures made. At one time, dentures were formulated from all kinds of things — horse teeth, or even illegally obtained ivory from harvested elephant tusks. Porcelain (and even wood) were also used to make dentures, but human teeth would have been the best materials with which to make prosthetic teeth. A good "doctor" with good tools might be able to do a nice side business making these (sometimes also harvesting the gold fillings from the recently deceased).

26. In fact, the earliest known copy of these works dates only from 1849.

SELECTED BIBLIOGRAPHY AND FURTHER READING

Association of Canadian Archivists Public Awareness Committee. *Aboriginal Archives Guide*. Canadian Church Historical Society Paper 8. Ottawa: Association of Canadian Archivists, 2007.

Bergey, Lorna L. "Contribution of the Mennonites to the Development of Waterloo County." *The Canadian Mennonite* 15, no. 24 (1967): 51–54.

———. "Early Mennonite Migrations from Pennsylvania and Subsequent Settlements in Canada." *Pennsylvania Mennonite Heritage* 9, no. 2 (1986): 2–12.

Bernier, Jacques. "Disease, Medicine and Society in Canada: A Historical Overview." The Canadian Historical Association, Historical Booklet 63. Ottawa: Canadian Historical Association, 2003.

Bloomfield, Elizabeth. *Waterloo Regional History Bibliography System*. Kitchener, ON: Waterloo Regional Heritage Foundation, 1993.

———. *Founding Families of Waterloo Township, 1800–1830*. Waterloo Township History Project. Guelph, ON: Caribou Imprints, 1995.

———. *Waterloo Township Through Two Centuries*. Waterloo, ON: Waterloo Historical Society, 1995.

———. "Building Community on the Frontier: The Mennonite Contribution to Shaping the Waterloo Settlement to 1861." *Ontario Mennonite History*, no. 2 (1997): 38.

Brantford Local History Archival Collection Fonds, Brantford.

Brown-Kubisch, Linda. *The Queen's Bush Settlement: Black Pioneers 1839–1865*. Toronto: Natural Heritage Books, 2004.

Buehler, Allan. *The Pennsylvania German Dialect: Pennsylvania German-English Dictionary, and Pennsylvania German Proverbs and Sayings, and Short Conversations, with English Translation: Also the Life Story of a Pennsylvania German Boy Growing Up, and What Life Is Like as an Old Order Mennonite*. Cambridge, ON: self-published, 1977.

Campbell, A.D. "Waterloo Body Snatcher: Dr. Friedrich Christ, 1824–1876." *Waterloo Historical Society Annual* 77. Kitchener, ON: Waterloo Historical Society, 1989.

Conner, J.W. "Berlin of Yesterday: Historical Sketch." In *Hannes Schneider and His Wife Catharine Haus Schneider, Their Descendants and Times, 1534–1939*, compiled by Miriam Helen Snyder. Kitchener, ON: published by Miriam Helen Snyder, 1937.

Doering, J. Frederick. "Pennsylvania German Folk Medicine in Waterloo County, Ontario." *Journal of American Folklore* 49, no. 193 (July–September 1936): 194–198.

Dunham, Mable. *The Trail of the Conestoga*. Toronto: McClelland and Stewart, 1942.

———. *Grand River*. Toronto: McClelland and Stewart, 1945.

———. "Waterloo County House of Industry and Refuge." *Waterloo Historical Society Annual* 35. Kitchener, ON: Waterloo Historical Society, 1947.

Eby, Ezra. *From Pennsylvania to Waterloo: A Biographical History of Waterloo Township*. Berlin, ON, 1895.

Ellis Little Papers. Ellis Little Room, Waterloo, ON, Public Library.

Epp, Frank. *Mennonites in Canada*. Toronto: Macmillan Canada, 1974.

Epp, Marlene. "Midwife-Healers in Canadian Mennonite Immigrant Communities: Women Who 'Made Things Right.'" *Histoire Sociale/Social History* 40, no. 80 (2007).

Good, E. Reginald. Editorial. *University of Waterloo Gazette*, October 25, 1995.

Good, Reginald. "Mississauga-Mennonite Relations in the Upper Grand River Valley." *Ontario History* 87, no. 2 (1995): 155–172.

Graeff, Arthur D. "The Pennsylvania Germans in Ontario, Canada." *Pennsylvania German Folklore Society Annual Yearbook* 11: 1–80. Allentown, PA: Pennsylvania German Folklore Society, 1946.

Haldane, E. Anne. *The Historical Geography of Waterloo Township, 1800–1855*. Hamilton, ON: McMaster University, 1963.

Hand, Wayland D., ed. *American Folk Medicine: A Symposium*. Berkeley: University of California Press, 1976.

Hele, Karl S., ed. *Lines Drawn Upon the Water: First Nations and the Great Lakes Borders and Borderlands*. Waterloo: Wilfrid Laurier Press, 2008.

Hoffman, W.J. "Folk Medicine of the Pennsylvania Germans." *Proceedings of the American Philosophical Society* 26, no. 129 (January–July 1889): 329–352.

Hohman, John George. *Pow-Wows, or Long Lost Friend*. Reading, PA, 1856.

Jaffray, William. "A Day at the Waterloo Poor House and What I Learned." *Waterloo Historical Society Annual* 57. Kitchener, ON: Waterloo Historical Society, 1969.

Johnson, Mary A. "A Brief History of Elementary Education in the City of Waterloo." *Waterloo Historical Society Annual* 53. Kitchener, ON: Waterloo Historical Society, 1965.

———. *The Trail of the Slate: A History of Early Education in Waterloo County, 1802–1912*. Waterloo, ON: self-published, 1975.

Johnson, Steven. *The Ghost Map: The Story of London's Most Terrifying Epidemic and How It Changed Science, Cities and the Modern World*. London: Riverhead Books (Penguin Group), 2006.

Jorgensen, Danny L., and Lin Jorgensen. "Social Meanings of the Occult." *The Sociological Quarterly* 23, no. 3 (Summer 1982): 373–389.

Kessler, Karl. "Mennonites and Milling in Waterloo Region." Mennonite Heritage Portrait. Accessed September 30, 2018. mennoniteheritage-portrait.ca/Report.php?ListType=Documents&ID=2148.

King George III of England. *Royal Proclamation of 1763*. collectionscanada.gc.ca/publications/002/015002–2010-e.html.

King, William Lyon Mackenzie. *Diaries of Prime Minister William Lyon Mackenzie King.* Library and Archives Canada.

Kohli, Marjorie. "The Coombe in Hespeler: Smyly Homes." *Waterloo Historical Society Annual* 80 (1992).

Kriebel, David W. *Pow-Wowing Among the Pennsylvania Dutch: A Traditional Medical Practice in the Modern World.* Philadelphia: Pennsylvania State University Press, 2007.

Lamb, Kathryn Hansald. "Restoration of the Waterloo County Gaol and Governor's House, Kitchener." *Waterloo Historical Society Annual* 89 (2001).

Letters to Christian Eby, ca. 1890–1920. Christian Eby Papers. Conrad Grebel College, University of Waterloo.

Library and Archives Canada. "Censuses." Online at bac-lac.gc.ca/eng/census/Pages/census.aspx.

Liebbrandt, Gottlieb. *Little Paradise: The Saga of the German Canadians of Waterloo County, Ontario, 1800–1975.* Kitchener, ON: Allprint, 1980.

Little, Ellis. "The Kitchener-Waterloo Orphanage Society." *Waterloo Historical Society Annual* 86 (1998).

Loewen, Royden. *From the Inside Out: The Rural Worlds of Mennonite Diarists, 1863 to 1929.* Winnipeg: University of Manitoba Press, 1999.

London Free Press. "Schoolhouse Built 130 Years Ago Still Stands." October 28, 1950.

MacRae, Ian J., and Linda Hutchison. "A Unity of Varied Particulars: Land, Language, Politics and History in Finding Common Ground." *Journal of Canadian Studies* 46, no. 2 (Spring 2012): 5–25.

Maines Pincock family fonds. Special Collections, Doris Lewis Room, University of Waterloo.

McKegney, Patricia. *Charm for Me, Mr. Eby: Folk Medicine in Southern Ontario 1890–1920.* Bamberg Heritage Series, no. 1. St. Jacobs, ON: Bamberg Press, 1989.

Mills, Rych. *Victoria Park: 100 Years of a Park and Its People.* Kitchener, ON: Victoria Park 100th Birthday Historical Committee, 1996.

Miloff, Allan. "Reminiscences of Life in Willow Hall, Waterloo." *Waterloo Historical Society Annual* 86 (1998).

———. "The Kitchener-Waterloo Orphanage Society." *Waterloo Historical Society Annual* 86 (1998).

Nyce, James M., ed. *The Gordon C. Eby Diaries, 1911–13: Chronicle of a Mennonite Farmer*. North York, ON: The Multicultural Historical Society of Ontario, 1982.

———. "Convention, Power and the Self in German Mennonite Magic." Ph.D. thesis, Brown University, 1987.

Page, F.E. "Homer Watson." *Waterloo Historical Society Annual* 32 (1944).

Pearce, Thomas. "School History, Waterloo County and Berlin." *Waterloo Historical Society Annual* 2 (1914).

Revie, Linda. "A Community Orphanage: Matrons and Benefactors." *Waterloo Historical Society Annual* 93 (2005).

Reaman, G. Elmore. *The Trail of the Black Walnut*. Toronto: McClelland and Stewart, 1965.

Reimensnyder, Barbara. *Powwowing in Union County: A Study of Pennsylvania German Folk Medicine in Context*. Vol. 31 of *Immigrant Communities and Ethnic Minorities in the United States and Canada*, edited by Robert J. Theodoratus. New York: AMS Press, 1989.

"Reminiscences of David B. Schneider, November 22, 1928." In *Hannes Schneider and His Wife Catharine Haus Schneider, Their Descendants and Times, 1534–1939*, compiled by Miriam Helen Snyder. Kitchener, ON: Miriam Helen Snyder, 1937.

"Reminiscences of Louisa Schneider Troxel." In *Hannes Schneider and His Wife Catharine Haus Schneider, Their Descendants and Times, 1534–1939*, compiled by Miriam Helen Snyder. Kitchener, ON: Miriam Helen Snyder, 1937.

Rogers, Edward S., and David Smith, eds. *Aboriginal Ontario: Historical Perspectives on the First Nations*. Toronto: Dundurn, 1994.

Roper, Jonathan, ed. *Charms, Charmers and Charming: International Research on Verbal Magic*. New York: Palgrave Macmillan, 2009.

Roth, Lorraine. "The Years of Benjamin Eby, Pioneer Leader in Ontario, Canada." *Pennsylvania Mennonite Heritage* 9, no. 2 (1986): 18–41.

Sokvitne, Miriam Snyder, "The Waterloo County Gaol: 1853–1977." *Waterloo Historical Society Annual* 65 (1977).

Steckle, John. "John Steckle Recollects." *Waterloo Historical Society* 53 (1966).

Still, William. *The Underground Rail Road.* Philadelphia: William Still, 1872. Reprint, Medford Township, NJ: Plexus Publishing: 2005.

Stowe, Harriet Beecher. *Uncle Tom's Cabin*. Cleveland, OH: Jewett, Proctor and Worthington, 1852. Reprint, New York: Dover, 2005.

Stroh, Jacob G., and Joseph M. Snyder. "Reminiscences of Berlin (Now Kitchener)." Parts 1 and 2. *Waterloo Historical Society Annual* 18 and 19 (1930 and 1931).

Thiessen, Paul, and Anne Eby Millar, eds. *"Of Course I Was Only an Onlooker": The 1911–1919 Diary of Gordon Christian Eby, Mennonite Farmer*. Kitchener, ON: MLR Editions Canada, Pandora Press, 2007.

Uttley, William (Ben) Velores. *A History of Kitchener, Ontario.* Waterloo, ON: The Chronicle Press, 1937.

Walker, James W. St. G. *"Race," Rights and the Law in the Supreme Court of Canada: Historical Case Studies. Waterloo, ON: Wilfrid Laurier University Press, 1997.*

Waterloo Chronicle. "Rich History to First Schoolhouse." February 10, 1988.

Waterloo Chronicle-Telegraph. May 28, 1903.

Waterloo County House of Industry and Refuge Register/Register of Paupers, Vagrants, & Idiots Received at the House of Industry and Refuge: 1869–1936. Waterloo Region Archives.

Weekly News-Record (Berlin, ON). Obituary of Levi Carroll. July 22, 1897.

Wells, Clayton W. "A Historical Sketch of the Town of Waterloo, Ontario." *Waterloo Historical Society Annual* 16 (1928).

White, Randall. *Ontario 1610–1985: A Political and Economic History*. Toronto: Dundurn, 1985.

Winks, Robin W. *The Blacks in Canada: A History*. Carleton Library Series 192. Montreal: McGill-Queen's University Press, 1997.

Wintemberg, W.J. *Folk-Lore of Waterloo County, Ontario*. National Museum of Canada Bulletin 116, Anthropological Series 28. Ottawa, ON: National Museum of Canada, 1950.

Wood, Louis Aubrey. *The War Chief of the Six Nations: A Chronicle of Joseph Brant*. Toronto: Glasgow, Brook, 1914.

Young, James. *Reminiscences of the Early History of Galt and the Settlement of Dumfries, in the Province of Ontario*. Toronto: Hunter, Rose, 1880.

Zavaros, Margaret. "Waterloo Park 1890–1990." *Waterloo Historical Society Annual* 78 (1990).

IMAGE CREDITS

Cambridge Archives: 31
Geoffrey Hayes, *Waterloo County: An Illustrated History*, 1997: 90
Kitchener Public Library: 12, 57, 80, 93, 100, 135, 152
Mennonite Historical Society Archives: 133
Muddy Creek Farm Library, Ephrata, Pennsylvania: 22
University of Waterloo, Maines-Pincock Photograph Collection: 147
Waterloo Historical Society: 28, 39, 42, 50, 54, 166
Waterloo Region Generations: 37, 88
Wellington County Archives: 61

INDEX